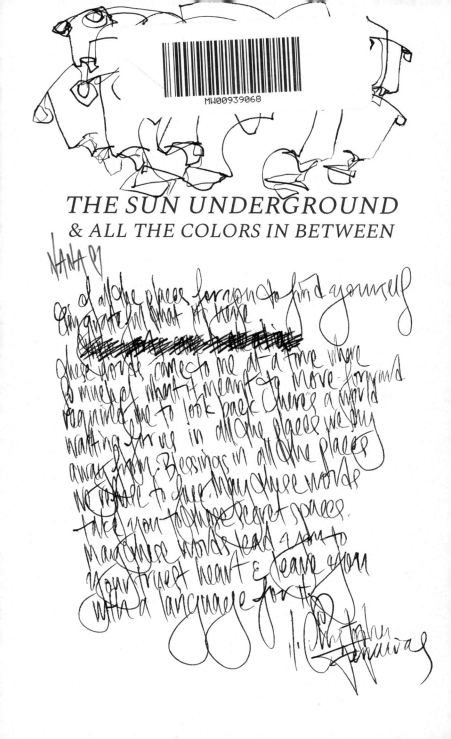

THE SUN UNDERGROUND
& ALL THE COLORS IN BETWEEN

THE SUN UNDERGROUND
& ALL THE COLORS IN BETWEEN

poems and not poems
with christopher ferreiras

CIELO SOL Y MAR

pa mi familia
Icarus

uelo uela
y ma

based on untrue told stories & the untold true

there are no sinners or saints here/
everyone is both/

by the time you are done/
you will be neither/

conócete

like a voice needs the quiet to find itself in us/
touch needs that small space between skins
to be touch/ silence as necessary to the song

as distance is to sensation/ as the horizon
between seconds rhymes breath to heart/
to make peace of panic/ beats of the beating/
music of noise & numb into feeling/

don't you hear it/
the way you are already music
in this life?

in the mourning/ the feathers fallen/
in the light of day/ how many lives
wait in the wings/ to turn burning
into shining & find flight in the falling?

las alas en la hora cero/
infinity in the zero hours/
a dios y las olas in the evenings/
a here so now it is already gone/
the moment, a season in itself/

can't you hear it/
how night is indigo so you can feel it/

our hymn at dawn/
your name in everything?

contents

MOURNING/   1-52

LIGHT OF DAY/   53-104

LA HORA CERO/   105-152

NIGHT IS INDIGO/ 153-200

DAWN/   201-247

MOURN·ING/
/ˈmôrniNG/

moments after dawn, before the blues brighten & the colors change, I find it hard to believe it is not still yesterday. the walls in my room the perfect shade of "too late for rest." too late to sleep without risk of missing the alarms. from this deep altitude, the day ahead steepens & I regret looking for whatever it was I thought I'd find after midnight/ whatever it was I was looking for. condemn the lights that kept me up. curse the scrolling curse the screen curse the urge to seek origin after origin. remembering. memory. grief is regret/ sadness/ or remorse about the loss or disappearance of a thing. or so they say. I know it as I do the morning—a point of no return. longing, sorrow, missing of the missing. reaching for a name & finding it isn't there. a yearning for what does not make it. the feeling that something there/ will make it easier to be here. is what got me here in the first place.

salt/

had Eve not been warned
& Orpheus gone uncautioned/

if Icarus wasn't told
& I urged you not to/

would you eat from my hands/
would you turn back/

& fall for me?

you choose the light you die for/

you choose
the light you die for
or find your way without it/

for every sun we miss another also rises,
for every light we lose another life opens/
& we lose our lives to what we don't do/

no loss makes you suffer/ quite
like the ignorance & wonder
of what would've been & become of you
in light of an unknown fire/

heavier than the heaven too hot to touch
horizon lost haunting your wings like waves/
wax in your eyes & salt in your lungs/
is drowning day after day dreaming/
about the way you could have flown/

there is no such thing
as flying too close to the sun/
you either burn for what you love/
or you watch somebody else/

nothing kills like a life you didn't live/
a story more day dream than yours to tell/

even the sun is in the dark/ that's why we see it

there is a damage in the distance
I have no intention of coming back from/

the thought I deserve exactly what's coming
keeps me going/

to get there before I catch myself.

I'm dying to know who I am/

these eyes grow darker by the hour/
& I'm afraid this old soul's catching up with me/

the thought you see too much/ you've seen it all/
could just mean it's time for a new mirror/
a new room/ a new view/

but I don't know. every blink leaves me smaller/
like I only just got here & just like that I am ancient too/
like it was only this morning we were born
yet we've been out here & at this
longer than I can remember + before/

there are times I want to be ash/ others
where I'm okay waiting in the wings/
burning a little longer/
so others may find their way/

sure I can't be the only one,
but one look & it looks like I am/
why does it feel like I am/
the only one/ dying to know who I am/
the only one/ wide awake & still
waiting to wake up/

alive/ in a life/ I can finally call mine/

lasting/

you have survived so many of my seasons/
where such parts of me have not.

I have been so many faces/
& you've held me through all of them/

fragile horizon/

there is a fine line/
between getting close to someone to be with them/
& being with them to get away from yourself/

fragile horizon/
these bodies/ this flesh/ this skin/
can't be all that keeps us here like this/

too much light/

seeing you go
stayed with me

is that what you meant/
when you said you'd never leave/

I close my eyes & still see yours/

we were so beautiful before/

maybe we are never more in love/
than moments before our awareness of it/
& we were so beautiful before/

yet you mourn the past life like it is still there/
how it remembers you/ not quite as you left,
but only how you left it & what you mourn is not that/
but to go back with these hands that know better now/
armed with a heart that finally knows how to have/

years & years/ are more you colored than me/ I grey looking
for something more lush than these lashes/ more blush
than the salt roses on my cheeks/ I hear *you* when *I* speak/
& yet it makes me lose sleep/

these haunts to piece together your voice from each letter &
text/ your scent to garment/ a fragrance more your voice than
mine/ to hear *you* speak again/ *I swear I was listening*/ a single
sentence is all I seek/ some semblance that I did not make you
up/ & if at all I was crazy it was for you, not about us/

your breath must still be there in the old library/ where you
let me show you how to breathe/ through chaos & anxiety/ you
cried & I kissed your eyes dry/ like a page absorbs rain & yellows
rather than tears/ what fears fell out your mouth/ I placed down
gently/ so you could see, these skies we bear may be heavy,
but not all that thunders crashes/

sometimes peace is the release of what we bury & it's too easy
to say the past is the past when you can't shake the sense that
something's missing & can't place what or where it was last/
there's something you're forgetting/ in spite of reality restored
'round your periphery/

I'm afraid there is nothing to go back to/ nothing to dig up/
unearth/ exhume/ it is where we're going/ & I wonder
if there's a sliver of silver in this for clouds of our kind/

if anyone ever gets back what they lost without finding
they never needed it/

yet you mourn the past life like it is still there/ tell yourself
if you could have it all again you'd have it all again
like you will never have it again. wouldn't change a thing
that happened. do it all the same just go about it a little
different. only a little. hold on a little longer.
breathe a little deeper. listen a little closer/

aware of the pieces you did not catch/ breathe them in
& prevent the sentences from failing/ miss the way
she looked at you & the way you saw this coming/

oh, we were so beautiful before/
maybe we knew it/ how we needed to/

& maybe it's best we don't know why/
now that we know better/

I may never know what you remember/

you only remember so much/
when the other half of your memories
isn't in your life anymore/

& I think isn't it funny when the one
who took you out of the picture
wants to know which ones you've kept/

forgive every blink/

past forgive me for the ways
I could not be present/

I listened as intently as one could/
all ears & eyes/ shoulder & spine/
I held on as long as the world would allow/

pardon every blink/
every stray of a wandering mind/

forgive me, past/
forgive me, for all the ways
I could not be present/

I still missed what I missed/
I still miss what I miss/

you miss what's there looking for it/

the way a reverie of warmth takes you away from the sun/
disappears what's here with the thought of one's touch/
you miss what's there looking for it.

I pull myself through myself for the angel in the rough.
imagine tomorrow & pick my skin. imagine tomorrow
If I just unkept this color of us in the dark & let it spill.
if I just let myself be what I am with you without you.

for the softness in the rough, I pick where you last touched.
to feel what's there before it's here. to know what skins
before skin and dusts before dust. what hid in touch
before touch unhid us. like something before picked me,
I picked you. & I could disappear before just about anybody
but in your gaze not go unseen.

how could I resist when dipping my hands into a reverie
was to be in yours again. to mouth the iron in my bleeding,
to taste how softness is never lost in the rough.

still, the things that shall never be are the heaviest to let go of/
what never was. the future. to be here. the texture of a feeling
trying to feel it. define it. have it. how they numb, blend & blur
as you seek the clarity more clear than what's there/
& like this you miss what's here looking for it.

tell yourself/ you must be whole and here without the secrets
shadows keep in the dust of our bodies. present and free without
these skins we shed and relieve. return, releave. relief & release/

you don't need a thing you lose/
you don't need a thing you lose/

you have to believe/
you don't need a thing you lose/

the one who gets away never goes away/

the closure we need
is rarely the closure we get/

what moves you
is not what you want
desire or dream/

not what you seek
but your ignorance
of what that is/

not the chance
of having the thing
but the belief that it's there/

the possibility/
the reason/
to go the distance/

a portrait of Icarus as a boy/

when I remember I can't sleep
when I can't sleep
I remember/

how the ocean returns what you've given
by taking it away first

the tide pool beds I made at the beach
waves rushing out from under my body
the salt & sand like curious hands on a breeze
nameless creatures sculpting me
into a castle stranded at sea

chasing the cool of my own shadow
& the heat beneath my feet chasing me
the seagulls' cries/ daydreaming
do they remember where they lose their feathers
who saw me fall running toward the shore to collect them
if we ever met again would they recognize me as that boy

(the way I can't seem to forget the kid who stole my toy/
the bees & dragonflies, did she ever make it to China—
the beauty who dug a hole so deep I didn't see her leave/
where do all the friends & enemies we make at the beach end up/
do they also grieve the way we didn't get to say goodbye)

I imagine often how it must feel being forgotten/
if all the parents but mine came to collect their children
& I was left behind. the ocean my mother again
for a night. the crescent moon, my father. more present
than waning. if I would make it to morning.

would mama & papa raise the sun and come looking/
find me returning where I came from/ cleansed
into what I'm made of/

glass is still sand/

what's a castle worth
made so damn close to shore/
when high tide rises and the walls
can't take it anymore/

what good is a moat made of broken bottles/
when the only difference between sand
& glass is how they fall apart/

when time can only tell
what it takes to put back together
& what becomes of anything
in the heat & salt of a summer day/

these days/
it doesn't scare me much/

I have seen what the sea does to glass/
the way it surrenders. turns edge
to soft landing. these ends
so few dare to touch.
such places no one dares to go.

these days
it doesn't scare me much,

I just go to the river & break.

river break/

can you blame the river
for wanting to carry you to the sea?

devil dreams/

papi used to have these dreams.
over breakfast, pouring coffee into saucer to cool it,

he'd tell us el demonio wanted something from him.
death was always on his tail like a shadow at his heels

& I wonder still if that was an omen or a warning.
his way of telling us. what was coming.

the running away part a sign
that he would not be staying the following years.

as a boy I never dreamed of the love I arise beside now/
this girl I got/ brighter than venus & always up before me/

she does things I don't even think to do.
turns the milk to foam before pouring it into our coffee/

she's got this way of softening/
everything that's heavy/

over brunch, she doesn't notice the haunting.
either way I wouldn't know what to say.

I've been having devil dreams. death's been chasing me.
when I see whose face it is I wake up

& I think it's a little soon
to chase me out of this home already.

labyrinths/

when you learn your father
left behind a labyrinth/
it's hard not to become a maze
looking for reasons why/

/—Da(e)d(alus)/

how you are in everything I do
though you are not here—
I don't know/

even absence is a presence
when you can't understand why
someone you love has gone/

& I can't say what stings more deeply/ the pain of loss
or the thought you deserve it. but it is one hell of a labyrinth
to carry & live in/ this shadow of a man you can't escape
& would rather not become/

heavier shadow still/ to get to the center. reach the source.
unlearn what you've known, and embrace that a father's mistakes
are his mistakes/ his fates are his fates & yours are yours
as yours is your own.

so can you really fault Icarus for not listening to Daedalus?
when the man's gift was that he brought ruin to everything
he touched. was it truly so foolish after all
to fly so close to the sun

when resisting the mistakes
others make turns you into them
& resisting ruin ruins you too.

it's only betrayal if you don't see it coming/

day breaks with this sharp ache
too deep in me to reach/
I must have slept weird/

where you used to scratch
a knot at my wing now
when I breathe/

reminds me what it is/
to lose something
you thought you'd always have/

like falling asleep
on your back to prevent this sort of thing
only to wake up hurting again/

this wasn't supposed to happen again/

funny/ at breakfast,
the knife I used to crack my eggs
reminded me

in my dream/
we were still friends/

bad dream?

strange nightmare I keep having/
I keep having you & not having you/

ignorance is bliss/

hell is missing someone you can't tell/
knowing full well it is better this way/

& wishing you hadn't/

your name is a feeling/

what I dream I can't tell you.
how I feel I can't say. what I mean, it's too late.

do I dare disrupt your healing
to check if I am still a wound/

to scratch this itch & say I am sick
of acting like I don't care just to make you feel better/

I dizzy telling myself I am okay with this distance
when I'm not. what I am is tired. tired of seeming.
tired of pretending longing is growing pains/

do I dare send the message unsent
just to forget I don't have you near/

weakness or strength/

do you know what it is
to miss you & say nothing.
is it weak to stay away
or is this strength?

selfless selfish foolish or dishonest/
to do the right thing when I don't want to/

you forget/

damn tease to speak your name
and not taste you/

where a voice goes when you bite your tongue/

where does the voice go
when you bite your tongue?

I want to say/

the way you shut the door
says everything you've locked up/

but I don't know if you hear how

I didn't want out/
but you wouldn't let me in.

just because you let go
doesn't mean I did.

dark matter, darling/

how you breathe into a space/
what parts your lips & escapes

when you sigh rather than say/
stays & stays & *it stays/*

the voice unvoiced. moves like a noxious gas.
permeates the air like poison & suffocates just the same.

this quiet slithering unscented lingers
within the walls & slips through the cracks/

hides in your pockets & seethes in your eyes so ablaze
you can smell it like a carcass so rotten at the foundation
of your home it's almost alive/

the unsaid follows & grows in the bones of a certain silence/
listening. building up like oil turns to grime on the kitchen ceiling/

this well of unsaid things sets the tone/
where the tone of your thoughts paint what you see/

revealing in its weight a severity/ tension so thick a look alone
could cut it & there's something unsafe about seeing red
& exchanging niceties instead/

having to answer how your day went over dinner
as the dark matter feeds/ on what you intended before you black/

& that's why where a voice breaks tells the whole truth/
slammed doors, shattered plates, no way to speak/

but they say everything we meant/
when our tongues fall short of our words
& we just can't anymore/

repression/

be careful what you bury/
it just might grow/

you swear you burn bridges/

you swear by the embers you burn bridges/

yet you wait for what remains as the smoke clears
looking from here where waiting
is no different than staying/

you swear by the embers you burn bridges/

staring at the other side
waiting to find if what's there
is still looking for you/

& that's not quite burning the bridge is it?

that what you meant by lighting the way,
settling yourself in flames
so they can see you too?

error/

it wasn't my mistake to think you were different/
it was my mistake to think that I would be/

true colors/

how one paints their past
is how they will color you

the past is watching us repeat ourselves/

how you are here
should never have to do
with how long you've been here.

years & years don't mean a thing
when your heart's no longer in it.

staying is not proof of presence/
a shared past is no promise of lasting/
having history doesn't mean having to stay.

ephemera/

as if they'd seen all they needed to see
the first leaves to fall are those atop the trees/

reds orange yellow & plume through the green
revealing the secrets ether keeps & the catharsis underneath/

can't change who we've changed away from/
we need the seasons as we do the days/

what falls away from us/ our fall away from others/
springs us closer to ourselves/

& what better reason is there to feel
than the fact none of it ever lasts?

what you release releases you/

the test isn't questioning
what's holding you back, but letting it go
when you find the answer/

let go of what wants to be lost/

you can't salvage what wants to be lost/
gripping tighter is no way to feel
what's slipping away/

you will only end up crushing it.

the sky changes because we're breathing/

& maybe moving on is less about giving up
or letting go and more about making way.

letting in. letting happen.
opening. surrendering.

the hardest thing about letting go/

is not that you need this thing
you're holding onto, but facing
that you really don't.

you were fine before it,
you will be fine without it.

heaven only knows what happened here/

what were we if we can't tell a soul

if I never make a sound of our story
was it real if we don't talk about it

what happened here
if I can't say a word
about how gorgeous we were
without giving us away

the way you taught
me to love, nobody knows

this secret
is the only way
I get to keep us

you love what you want to know/

hard to trust someone who doesn't want to know
who you were before/

someone who loves what they know/ when they don't know
what they don't know/ to trust your heart in their hands
when they refuse to ask who had you then/ what it took
& what took them/

hard to trust someone who doesn't want to know who you were
before them & have to trust they are who they say they are/
that you'll be who you say you'll be/ when they'd rather not go
where you've gone/ or see what you've seen because it's easier/

& it's never easy to yield in love when you can't rest assured
that they'd love who you were in the past/ to play like you
could ever be a blank slate/ grieve the way you'll never see them/
& crave it just the same/ but in the beginning a place null
& void of yesterday always seems safe/

like what was has no place where you are/
has no place just because you don't want it there/
as if being without the past is being without a past
or even a sort of purity/

but there's no noise louder than history denied
to maintain a veil of silence/ no tapestry more fragile or chaos
more dangerous than false peace/ no pain quite like bearing
an untold story & having to live an omission/

as if what came before doesn't shape what's present/
I'm afraid no true purity is without the past. can't really say
what you have if you don't face there's no here now or today
that isn't also half yesterday/
& no tomorrow/

hard to trust someone who doesn't want to know
who you were before them/

anyone can take you as you are
if they're not willing to see who you've been/

& sometimes, that's more daunting
than liberating.

there are worse things than ending up alone/

maybe if you didn't hide
what you felt would hurt them/
they'd have to get used to it/

if they seem unable to live with it
or express no willingness to learn/
if they are more fear and urge to self preserve
than love dares to chase curious concern/
let them live without/

let them learn
to live with the truth of who you are/
without you/ if they can't seem to/

because that can't be love/
to fear losing them so much
you can't even be honest/

slant of light/

once you said/
sometimes you have to live a lie
so others remember it as the truth.

& I'm trying to recall
when you started loving me less
& starting to wonder if you ever loved me at all.

desire never gets old/

you never stop wanting
what you could not have/
until you have it/

& desire never gets old/
it gets tired but it never gets old/

all these years/ they keep up. shadowing
the little things you still want. what you haven't had/
what you had & all that wouldn't let you/

desire never gets old/ chasing gold to curse
the ones who never treasured your touch/

but punishment is an answered prayer & promises
just have this way of getting us into things we can't keep/

& it's too easy to forget how you wanted what you have
when you don't want it anymore/

can't play like you didn't prey
on what you're trying to get away from now/

that you are over it/
does not mean desire ever gets old/

the want never goes away, what you want just changes/
you don't need what you used to & what you need
to affirm your having, that changes too/

but desire never gets old/

change for me so I can feel better about loving you/

when a bird of prey loses a feather on one wing,
it pulls a feather from the other to even out
its grace & fly more steadily.

& I think one can only do this
and call it balance so often/
before they're all out of feathers to pull/

human/

love is not possessive. we are.

look at us/ trying to keep this like it's ours
just because we have it now. look at us compromise/
like compromising in love doesn't compromise the love.
look at us/ we've got love all wrong with need/

mistaken attachment as selfless & caring
for the precious as license to keep/

maybe what we think is us in love is us in fear/
maybe everybody's afraid to lose what's theirs
because no one's really sure they have it/

maybe no one really leaves you
because they were never really yours keep/

& maybe this is why we try at keeping/

because we only try to keep what we're afraid of losing/
not what we're sure is ours or for us/

love is not possessive. we are.

& I don't know if you can have anything purely
if you're afraid of losing it/ I don't know
if anyone who's really sure of what they have
or is secure in what is theirs/ is afraid to lose it/

but I swear this impossibly strong and fragile thing
between us is real & I don't want to love the way I do
but I'm afraid to lose you/

so what does that make me?

if it is love let it be love/

if it is love, do not be sorry.
if you feel a will to give your all & all to give
what does it matter that another did not ask for it?

this energy. this awakening. might feel because of them
but it is not about them. for them is always for you/
the way you love is who you are.
the way you love is who you are.

& this way you are is about you.
this surrender, flow & flourishing/
its life is as it is for its own sake.

& so few can tell the difference
between what they know and need.
can anyone really say what they want?

seasons come and go as do we. want more & need less.
days where nothing is enough & nothing is just fine.
then there are those who seem like seasons but last lifetimes.
those who miss the world right in front of them looking for it.
& that's them. that's who they are.

don't torture yourself thinking about who looks
but doesn't see you. those who hear but don't understand.
don't torture yourself thinking you shouldn't have
when you had it in you to share.

better that you aren't losing sleep wishing you would have/
could have done more. it is not on you that they didn't know
how to hold it all. their hands may have felt enough to touch you,
but such hands weren't enough if they couldn't stand
the ways you didn't hold back.

so don't hold back now.
if they miss the heart set loose,
at least the wind will catch it.

if it is love,
let it be, love/

above all/

love like no one asked for it/
because nobody's asking
but everyone deserves it/

love like you have everything
to give & nothing to lose/
because you do.

what the mirror sees/

how clearly you could see what was
when it's not that way anymore/

where you were
when you are no longer there/

look back & admit to grace, alignments & moments
rhyming/ all within purpose & reason alike/

what beauty you couldn't see
at the time/ the softness in the rough/

how odd remembering/ all we've been
through, what little I recall now/

& how lucid I am
about what was & wasn't/

how clear that
it had to be us/

forgive yourself/

forgive yourself/ for all you gave & can't get back/
forgive yourself/ for all you did not give/
forgive yourself for what you did not catch/
& stop trying to catch lies with the very hands
that let go of the ones who told them/

forgive yourself for the scars/
for thinking it would make you feel better
to pick the scab & beat them to the pain
in case they ever try you again/

forgive yourself/ for falling for what was not there/
stand strong against that small fall over your belly
that wants to get even & forgive yourself
for wanting to break them the same way
you feel broken/ so they can hurt as you hurt/

you hurt yourself first before hurting anyone else/
forgive yourself for doing as they did just to see
if you have it in you & doing damage to someone
who didn't deserve it/ because nobody deserves it/
not them/ not you.

forgive yourself for not forgetting. forgive yourself for needing
time & distance. to trust again. to believe again. to let in again.
to forgive yourself/ forgive yourself/ for not forgiving yourself/
even if you said you did/ forgive yourself for saying you let go
even if you haven't couldn't or didn't/ forgive yourself/

for being unable to unsee them in light of how you've seen them.
for needing a chance to outrun their shadow.
forgive yourself for forgiving them.

in spite of the old ways,

for opening the blinds & letting in new light.
for breathing the final inhale before lifting open
the windows & releasing the final exhales
of their being there. for seeing the damage done,
embracing the ruin & walking through it.

forgiveness means you don't use one's past
to justify your present transgressions.

tracing the trails to the sources of what happened/
and leaving behind the skins shed & past lives.
it means they stay, where you keep going.
& you always keep going.

when it's us, it's us/

we all wake up from dreams of falling/
before we reach the earth/

for every sun gone underground
another is unearthed/

& for every cloud you fall through/
there's a dream bound to catch you/

they are nothing to mourn/
feelings nothing to grieve.

don't you feel how it all changes
as we breathe?

how there's more sky
where we come from/

always more sky
where we come from/

LIGHT OF DAY/

*from atop the tower, sights set over the sea, the ingenious artist &
giver of wings woke the boy and said it's go time. careful, he warned.
the sun rises faster than it seems. fly too high and the wax will
melt. too low and the salt will turn your wings to stone. today, we
say something that does not see the light of day goes unknown. it
might as well not exist. I think of what it means to write this. to
be brought out of hiding. to meet a sky after captivity & seem so
close to being alone with the thing burning in heaven. if for a brief
moment, to those who bore witness, his flight looked like he made
it. if anyone but his father even noticed. did crashing through the
trembling flames blazing on the face of the ocean feel like tearing
through the sky to the otherside/ was breaking through the liquid
gold just to ripple with it worth drowning? imagine/ what this could
have meant to the father before triumph became failure & his son's
plummet, a lesson. on the sun underground into the city, I think of
what becomes of secrets taken to the grave. voices unvoiced & stories
gone untold. tales we don't get to tell ourselves. the difference in how
things would've unfolded. I think of what it means to write this. how
unideal a time morning was for flying. how unideal a time morning
is for anything. if the boy thought this too.*

mass/

you will always be too much
for someone who isn't enough
for themselves/

you are too much to feel so little/

measure/

if I must be made smaller
so you may hold me
do you really have me?

temperature/

whatever texture or weight
feels most true to you is okay/

if sensitivity is your wealth
& feather softness your resilience/

if collapse is how you find your strength/
do not harden or be disheartened/

cold heart of steel or heavy heart of stone/
both are still made of warmth/

those who don't feel you
won't feel you anyway/

& not everyone needs to.

CHRISTOPHER FERREIRAS

feeling is being/

never make yourself lighter
because others can't bear
the weight of your world/

never compromise your texture
because some body can't handle
the way you feel/

the dark is proof you are here/

we've got such parts about us
these parts that want to be seen & known
these parts that want to be left alone
these parts that are never not alive
with the burning or blooming

these parts stand side by side
as we do our own dark places
they come together to make us
stand out against the substance
of what can't be seen with eyes open

when you reflect
you see what's missing
so many spaces left to fill
all this empty & no place to begin
but do not shy where you are darkest
& face your shadow

how can you feel anything
less than full?

anything short of endless.
complete. whole. v a s t.

infinite

oil on canvas of whatever you want me to be/

not what you spirit into the dark,
but what makes it to the other side/

not what you lose in the looking
but every turn a labyrinth *takes*
so you can find/

something as light as the sun on one's shoulders
can be one hell of a world on another's back/

how you see me
depends on the light you carry.

morning star/

why is it so easy for you to hear the sun
when another's mouth spills with shadows
but not when you speak?

you have so much to your name
how can you only hear it
when someone else says it?

why can't you hear it
if no one else does?

crimson/ vermillion--I forget the difference/

you are too deep a color
to play inside all the time

afraid to bleed is no way to live
holding back is no way to hold
& afraid to feel is no way to touch/

haven't you seen how the sun cries

what paintings it makes of the sky
the colors it spills into the ocean
& forgets the horizon line

kissing your skin?

eggshells/

everything I touch
breaks me a little.
that's how I feel it.

who wins
when you love
so carefully?

fire-shy/

in she walks and out goes reason/
with it goes my words/

like a spark burns brightest
before its light's out/

& the black of blinking
reveals its color/

eyelids heavy when we must tear away/
from what reminded us of such gravity/

tongues cotton afraid to speak/
& all that's left is embers & remembering/

still falls the flame reaching for the source
of this passion that lit it. the answer in the ashes.

like wax is shy of fire, triumph
& tragedy shy of each other

even if we are not/ afraid of getting
burned something in me melts

reaching for what the dark
call the stars between us.

if you see something say something/

say nothing long enough
almost begins to taste like you said
what you meant to say/

so take it from a stranger
who has lost more magic to the hope of finding it again
than he's ever dared to seize it while he could/

when I say that if your eyes meet a soul so bold
she looks you in the face and does not shy away/
say something/

the one who gets away never goes away
& believe me you never stop wishing
you said something/

you can try to recreate today tomorrow/
take the train at the same time
in which you saw her/ stand exactly
where you stood/ play yourself to the thought
that drawing her from memory is the same
as writing her name & number/

but you will only be standing there praying
for another chance/ telling yourself this time/
next time you would/ you will/ you shall/

but you don't. you cannot recreate fate/
or a chance which is yours to take/
some trains just aren't for you to make/
even when you're on it/

but if you're on it
& you see something

say something/

snitch on the heart/
give it what it wants even if it hurts/
it will thank you later for the pain/

because the pain
that you were only a word away
from what could've been

is more punishing
than saying the wrong thing

or not saying a thing at all.

here's a view/

what you can't quite see really makes you look/
& I don't think it's a mistake we blur the closer we get/

here's a view/

those closest to you are too close
to see where they are/ they forget

going through what you've been through,
the way they listened to get here

& that to be heard is to be seen/
to look to listen/ to listen to see/

& that's how we get louder, don't we/
lose sight of the forest for the trees/
the climb for the canopy?

swear we're being ignored/ aren't being heard/
what we don't voice growing ever louder/

spare another the bite in your damage
& only you feel the pangs of living
with what never happened/

sever the voice & your bones vibrate
with what you should've proclaimed/

no one else may have ears for it/
the hornet's nest in your throat, but it's there/

like a poem is the quiet screaming only you can hear/
loud, no doubt/ but never as loud as voicing what you need
when you mean it & what you mean when you need to/

gold is no less & no more the dirt where it's found/

bruised fruit have the most flavor/
& not everyone's been through what it takes
to savor the difference/

let no one into your garden
if they can't appreciate your roots/

they have no right to your fruit
if they won't get dirty to trace
what you've been through/

petals/

there was a rumor of Spring in the hills.
the trails half marsh & still quite snowed in/
when we found what could've been a flower?

you asked me what I want
& I don't know

how to say
if you must ask
you already know the answer/

you insist/

if you believe in what you love
& love what you believe in,
why are you so afraid of having it.
where's your faith in yourself?

but when you have a tendency to drop everything
you've picked up like it never even happened/
seems like the only thing you can't drop
is this bad habit/

I bring to your attention the thing/
there on the branch between grey & a hint of pink/
open & closed/ wonder if you're thinking
what I'm thinking/ feeling which the petals
I'm pulling/ if the bud was too early or too late/
or just petrified to commit/

you ask me why/

but if I must explain/
I don't think you'd get it/

don't you dare me/ I always choose truth

& it's a losing game/

to think anyone can complete you
when they are puzzled with the pieces
in themselves/

the last to know are always the last to know/

no one can hurt you quite like someone
who knows more about you
than they allow you to know about them/

at times you look at me/
words slow as I watch you speak,
and I could swear I don't really know your name

& everyone's in on it.

no one can hurt you quite like someone
who knows more about you
than they allow you to know about them/

lovers are always the last to know
where our hearts truly are
how conditional our love truly is.

makes a difference/

you saw yourself in the clouds
& she saw herself in the rain/

what set you apart/

is that everything she's done for herself
she did with you in mind/

and you only do it with you.

we grew in love & in love we grew/

maybe we did not fall from the same height/
but we ripened in each other's hands/
blossomed in each other's touch/

& that is just as sweet/
just as delicious/

& just as right/

between falling & wanting to/

there's falling
& then there's wanting to/

& here we go pretending
we can stop ourselves
even if we tried/

and you didn't see this coming?

what hurts
is not that I didn't know
but that somewhere hidden away,
tucked deep in the ends
of your smile, I already knew.

ruin in the wings/

chase a horizon long enough/
you don't know how to have a sun
you don't drown for/

my gut tells me
we're not going to last,
but the rest of me wants to know why/

& I have a hard time believing
there isn't gold in being a fool/

that there can't be grace in ruin too/

***what you want is to be chasing/*

if you didn't think you needed the thing,
would you want it?

would you
want what you seek
if you didn't have to look for it?

would you
want what you're chasing
without the chase?

say the sun & whatever it's hiding
were right there, would you reach out
to the horizon line & pull?

or do you need to fall
to know what you're worth?

if you lost me you never had me/

she shows you exactly how to love her/
you lack attention, not ability/
you forget & you lose her
every time you don't notice/

the red string out of the maze is not a loose thread

how they will treat you/

pay close attention
to how they treat
what they don't want anymore

dark third/

I've been the shadow of a father's warning
& the fire of unsorry stars

I've been the ocean & the maze
the men & the monsters

I've been afraid of becoming
the kind I warn you about

I often wonder which side sent me
but I've been the devil

& you can't make anyone
do what they weren't going to do already

you are what you recall & not at all/

can't quit the devil you keep choosing/
change your choices & your chances change with them.

they say the devil lies in the details,
but really the devil dwells in your patterns.

habits you no longer favor are no longer a choice,
they are a default setting. & that can be hell.

but observe where you default & what you fall for.
pay attention & judge if you must, but never condemn

what you are bound to
or yourself for being bound to it.

what haunts your body longs for the same freedom you seek.
like a shadow spills from your feet/ you are not alone

in your need to let go. so go there. where you can't help but fall.
stand tall beside yourself & have spirit/

be your own guiding hand
in deciding to choose otherwise/

you can't quit the devil you keep choosing/
until you choose to choose against what you've been

again & again.
& this can be change

if you let it/

y tu quien eres/

when there's a person you want to avoid
in a place you can't escape.

when that place is your own face.

they say I look like my mother,
why do I see my father?

a cautionary tale raised me/

so many ages trying not to be
what I swore myself
I'd never become/

I can't say whose life I've been living/
mine or unlearning what mazes
I've made of me/

trying to escape your fate/
I think I've become you
trying not to be you/

voice/

what's the use
of finding your voice
if you'll only speak
what others
want to hear?

in medias res/

remember in English, when we were kids? paired off
we'd read from the same book, the same page at a time.

without fail, there was always one person who finished
the page first & one who had to wait for the other to finish.

always fell heavy on me/ the page.
sharing words with someone else. having to. turn the page
when you're still trying to understand what you're looking for/
how you even got there. & have to again. turn the page. and pretend
you're reading the following line when your mind's still on the first.

how was it others could read so much faster than me.
maybe I was just the slowest reader ever. was the speed of reading
a sign of efficiency, was I slow or just thorough, I don't know.
I was never too sure. only that I liked to see how deep a word could
go and how far it could take me. how words hold within them other
words. the way meanings hold within them other meanings.
others' & our own.

the teachers would ask us about what we read.
questions curiosities concerns. predictions inferences new words.
nothing's ever too big or too small. but one only notices so much,
so that's concerning. you notice more together, but still you only
notice so much. it's impossible. to catch all that's going on in a
page. our answers always something different.
as were our questions.

curious. the way chapters & stories come to a close.
characters may finally touch there/ imagine what lies beyond the
spine/ let the mind wander off the edge of the line, dream about
what the sun hides, what a word isn't saying in what it does say.
what awaits when you step over the period.

but separate fates never meet on the same page.

the middle, merely a dream, never a promise.
the same ends, ending up together, rarely ever destined.
you strive to meet there. step over the period.
and hope whatever arises of trying
is both the destination & the right thing.

I don't know.
can't be too sure.
just my prediction.

what I do know/

there's always something/ some new change awaits
with every turn of the page. always someone
who reads for the lines and what lies between them.
one who reads the story to be with the words and one
who loses the lines just to reach the last verse.

always someone ready to move on to the next page,
next chapter, next story, and always someone who waits.

curious.

how you could be on the same page
with someone & still not be
on the same page/

stories/

knowing that we're merely the stories we tell
doesn't change our need to tell them.
to others. to ourselves.

this story. deepens & blooms as we do/
unfolds by way of what you seek
& what you're rooted in.

like a poem denudes the more you read it/
the more truth we choose to remember from shapes
the way history meets this moment
& what myth becomes of us/

the past changes from where you look/
upon whose eyes you welcome the future through/

this story you tell yourself of who you are matters/

more than the way others see you/
more than the way others saw you/
more than the way others don't/

say you were a siren that led some souls astray/
a persephone of false promises, eurydice or fury/
so what/ a narrative about you is only true if you believe it/

& every story is merely a side.

but this story you tell yourself/
who you are. none can author but you.

what happens/
tomorrow, only
yours to tell;

what you are no one can take from you/

what can you really take from me/
what do you have of mine
that I didn't let you have?

so you have a story. a memory of a time.
an example, an occurrence.
so you have a feather to my name.

you can't tell me who I am
or where I am going/
understand me/

you can't take a thing I gave you/
you may have something that was mine
but *I* gave it to you/ I let *you* have it/

understand me/
I do not need to be understood/
get me? you don't got me.

you know what to call me,
but that doesn't mean I'm looking/
a feather from my wing is not my wings/

not my flight. not my past.
not my sky. not my future.
no. my name is not my story.

& you may know it,
but you do not own me.

veritas/

in fact/
the truth does not hurt/

the broken lie hurts/
the illusion hurts/

that you thought it was the truth hurts/
that you couldn't see through it hurts/

that the truth hurts reveals more
about your reality than the truth itself/

that you couldn't see it wasn't
the truth hurts & then it will soothe you.

because the truth is, *the truth is*
while everything else is trying to be.

& that's how you know/
that's how you tell/

the difference is felt.

what then of the fires that need rescue from fading/

let's be honest. like the sirens
& red lights howl 'round our bedroom
to put out some fire down the street/
that could happen here.

there is a point of no return in all things.
one strikes a match/ it catches flame & shares the fire with
candle and curtain alike. one says too much/ gets caught in false
light & at some point the heat rises where it is too late/
what happened, so fast/ we only see it as a slow fade/

what seems to fade away/
is only the rest of a spark that stopped burning long ago/
the remains lingering long enough to let us watch & believe
there was a chance to pull the blinds before it started/

what happens to something you lose sight of before sight
of it is lost/ rest assured, there's still time to save it?
I am afraid that if you must do something about it
there is nothing to be done/

there is a point of no return in all things & it is crossed where
no one can see/ around the bend down the street/ as the howl
disappears & its echo is all that's left/ what was once sweet about
trying turns sour/ after years & hours of trying to revive a fire/
breathing life into the long expired/

what becomes of all the lost things?
when you were a kid & the balloon slipped out from under your
fingertips/ you see it going going gone until the crimson string
is lost beyond the clouds/ heaven only knows what happened/
where it ended up/ hands of an angel/ Icarus/ a past life/ a landfill/
or bound so tightly around a tree branch a Robin entangled dies
dangling waiting to be found/

let's be honest
like all the lost things
not even light can reach/

you forget how it feels to have what was yours
but you never quite forget how it feels to know
you'll never get it back & just like that/
nothing fades like a promise unmade/
nothing fades away like people/

I wander down the avenue/
try to gather what happened on that street/
daydream about the life you'd lead if I was not here/
& I want to see where you'd go if I just let you/
if such a living would bring you back to me/
if I didn't breathe life into this flame/

would I ever see you again
if I didn't ask first?

what then of the fires
that need rescue from fading?

where are you thinking from when you swear you're in love

you'd be surprised by what you miss
thinking you've seen it all/

you lose sight of who you are with
the moment you are without a doubt about them/

the moment you think you know someone better
than they know themselves you've lost them/

& you will never see who is in front of you
if you seek in them someone they are not/

but before you go grieving all the ways
you will never see what lies before your very eyes/
consider who you are with & who you are/

if you truly want them for them/
& if the future they're bound to
is one they'd value without you too/

or is what you want what you want/
do whatever it takes to have it/
even teach them how to fit the part?

what you have is false
when you love with the future
instead of your heart.

& there's nothing more violent
than loving someone for all that they're not/

& leaving for all they couldn't be for you/

forgive me/ I am not sorry

so forgive me/

I couldn't be as you imagined/
I can only be what I am/

forgive me/
I am not sorry/

only grateful/

no love more pure/

there is no love more pure
than being with someone
who does not need you/

which is to say they've seen
who you are through who
you think yourself to be/

& have chosen
to choose you/

mercy/ killing

when you don't talk to anyone
the way you talk to yourself/
that's both a mercy & a killing/

how you would defend yourself
from another is how you must
defend yourself from yourself/

from the vultures that pick you apart from inside out/
from the beasts that haunt the mazes of your mind/
the snakes that hiss in your silence & the wolves that howl/

you banish none of them/
you punish no one else/
so why do you punish yourself?

such mercies you reserve for others/
when your heart needs it too/

take the bravery & grace
what heart you have & keep it/

you deserve your mercy just as well/

man is a fragile state/

man is a fragile state/
boy, you can break/
it is okay/ it is okay
to not be okay/

no one is more fragile
than he who does not fall apart.

man is a fragile state
& this is okay.

boy, your hands are enough rough, picked sore
& still worthy of touch/ boy, you're allowed
to be in your skin/ let the world down a while/
to be your age/ your size/ your height/
your body/ is everything petal soft as is the heart.
your heart. is the only muscle that matters.

man is a fragile state/
boy, cloud is still a shape/
weep, rain if you will/
storm if you must to find calm/
there is strength in yielding.

man is a soft place/
boy you can break/
you're allowed to wilt/
fall into place.

consent/

surely your hands can be soft. careful. seeming
to know precisely where to go and what to do.
you can take a turbulent evening & tender her
goodnight. and it would not matter how gentle,
smooth, or good you think you are
if she does not want you touching her.

CHRISTOPHER FERREIRAS

you're no different/ I'm no better

hard to tell where our intentions begin
& where another's hands end.

to face what you want
when you're afraid of it.
to look & see what you're made of.
how you're not all that different
from those who took what they wanted.
not too far off from those who take
what becomes theirs.

you are capable/
of everything you swear you'd never.
the moment you swear you are good/
you are gone.

stare at the crossroads in the palms
of your hands long enough,
you start to get real curious
about where they've been
& what they've done.

who you were all along.

come back/

tell me it is not a shade of grace
the way you give wings to all you touch
& never ask a thing to stay/

turn skin to clouds
& neither ask for silver nor rain
not even a little sun in return/

what a violence, such a sweetness/

to fall for hands so selfless,
they aren't afraid of losing
what's theirs to see what they have

& hope you'll be the exception/

I almost feel wrong being so damn high
when my only wish was that
you would've asked me/

losses/

more than anything,
I don't fear loss, I fear
not knowing what I have.

because we can lose what we forget,
but we don't forget what we lose/

anybody can love you/

the truth is
anybody can love you.

but you have to want them to
and want them too.

I can't let go of your light/

life presents us with the past
to see if we're still there/

& though I still love with the same heart
that learned to love you, I'm wiser
from how I remember us/

wiser than nostalgia/
more aware than I wish I were,
but still aware/

far enough to feel
something is still there
close enough to know what never was/

I can't let go of your light/
but I don't have to/
to have to/

boundaries/

to take you with me/
without taking you away from yourself/
to lose myself with you without losing me/

boundless/

how the sun makes love to your face
& lets me watch/

show me what you love/
I'll meet you there.

LA HORA CERO/

before ma was my mother, she was a hunter. Papá taught her how to shoot a rifle when she was only a niña. to protect the family's livestock, they'd fire big birds out of the sky. before sunrise bled over God only knows where & the sun set en el campo where she grew up, Papá would light a cigarette as the gloaming tore over hills & mountains and the earth turned cold. the air a sort of silver. a hue of blue so in between hues everything blurred & your eyes almost hurt looking at anything too long. he called the evening la hora cero. ni de noche ni de dia. neither night nor day. neither here nor there.

in the hereness of it all/

there's just something about sunsets/
& watching beautiful things end
that makes you forget they're meaningless,
but that's everything/

the most beautiful things happen
when they don't have to/

all you are/

you exist to someone you didn't even notice/
someone you've never met remembers you/
a stranger wishes they knew your name/
you were the best thing that happened to them that day/
they think about you/ they pray they'll see you again/
they want another chance to say something/

matter/

you matter/
more than the way
you want to matter/

you matter more
than you know/

soma/

I want to say/ it does not matter/
what you have or where you come from/
all that matters is who you are/

but sometimes that feels like precisely the problem/

perhaps it is so that thinking is not quite living/
but then I think about it & have no doubt that life is
no more & no less in our heads than it is without/

it leaves me in knots/ the thought that we might not know we are
alive absent our minds/ the haunt that thinking is living when it
really isn't, but it really is/ what's not but could be/ being neither
here nor there & having to go outside when I'm already
everywhere from my bed/

now it's not that I don't want to see anyone,
it's that I don't want to be seen/ outside gets darker earlier
& colder sooner/ & sometimes all I want is to stay in bed all day
dreaming/ listening to the loudest possible music/ praying
for the loudest possible sound/ to put us all in our place/

for the mist to turn to rain & that the rain won't stop/
watch it cancel everything/ maybe then we'd get to meet the one
who banished us to *this*/ see I'd live accordingly
if I knew what it was all for/

I want to say this but can't have you thinking I am depressed/
make something up about something coming up instead/
but I think you see through me/

you say I must learn to let go & live in the moment,
but darling, that's just it/

there isn't a moment I don't live in/
trying to find a way to be here/

evening/

letting go is only half the release/
the other half is resisting what returns/

& half of what happens is what you allow/
the other is what you welcome/

the rest is surrender/

learning to dance with the past/
without being possessed to stay there/

but night breeds longing
& I'm still learning the steps
to stepping away for myself/

how to stop hosting ghosts
that only miss my skin
when the moon is on the rise

& the day turns cold/

gold for a broken bone/

who convinced us it is the sun that sets
when it is the earth that turns/ day into night/
day into night/ day in day out/ like an odd fool
who trades gold for a broken bone every time/

I hear fall leaves are most red when they're hung up on summer/
the way we are brightest when we'd do anything to last a little
longer/ revive ghosted promises when a relationship
is pretty much over/ try warm nostalgias
when autumn creeps closer/

but look how passionately clouds collapse color
when night's about to come/ turns pink plum
like a face holding a lungful of smoke in one breath/
venus doesn't flinch/ light steady set on me set on her/
& we've only got minutes before the sun and moon finish
this vespertine flirtation;

new jersey's white red & orange blues twinkle neon
over black water & I watch/ my feet dirty with twilight kisses
and starry river spit/ sirens howl in ways wind won't take me/
vibrations make me cringe/ my phone won't stop going off/
battery life low enough to cancel living alongside my plans/

wish it'd just slip out of my hands into the hudson/
but you know/ people to see, places to be, poems to write.
from the edge of the city, I find it so curious how alive
it all seems when a part of you wants to die;

(not in a sad way. just in like a there's so much I want to do and don't
know where to begin or why/ you know, kind of like when you're running
late to work & you'd rather get hit by a truck than lie. in like a why the
hell is it so hard to wake up everyday type of way, I mean, don't you ever
just wish your phone would brick so you won't have to say shit?)

stark, the contrast/ the moment from memory/
the city from its reflection in the river/
how bright the streets in the dark and dark the darkness
against the light/ strange, what juxtaposition does/
how those moments you wish it'd all just end
or leave you alone reveal the reasons to be here most/

blessed, the way these small lights we turn from
still reach out to us like we didn't turn away/
day into night/ day into night/ day in day out/

something about where the earth's set gives this sense
there's so much on the horizon when you were so sure
to be done/ like there is this part of you that is moon too.

no matter how dark it gets, more is always on the rise/
it knows the night is young & you've only just begun.

persona/

you become other people
for other people and wonder why
it feels like nobody sees you/

it doesn't matter who knows you exist
if you don't feel comfortable on your own/
present or alive alone/

it doesn't matter who sees you
or doesn't if you don't see who you are
when nobody's looking/

to the part of you that already knows/
A MIRROR IS NO PLACE FOR PERFECTION

do not confuse your wings for the world/
as wings of this world/

they are yours/ as is this skin/
and one day shall not be/

a mirror is no place for reflection/
take your body to the water & let it river/

trace the ripples/ face
the waves & wave with them/

half the sun of heaven is in the ocean/
to bathe in a current is to return to it/

to reflect in the depth
is to ascend/

remember
who you are/

is in everything under the sun
and without it/

the romance of indifference & chance/

it's like

everybody's saying love yourself
& nobody's showing you how.

this life/ your body/ tell me it isn't something else/
the way it takes the poison you give & gives you water/
you give it ash & it scabs the burns the scars
and histories/ like you never picked them/

sheds bitten lips to a certain softness/ always
returning you to your texture/ line your lungs with sulphur
& it gives you breath/ hold your breath/ it won't let you/

& this dance/ this alchemy/
hellbent & heaven sent survival of us/
is not the cosmic made conscious?

maybe this "self love" stuff is as inherent to us
as it is taught/ the fine line between lesson & mere reminder/
that you are at your highest & lowest regard always adored
& deserving by something in the body/

always shedding, always unfolding/ in spite of your attachments/
forever releasing all you're holding/ in spite of need ego fear/
want & grasp/ eternally revealing eternally returning/
in spite what you've become/ the body heart & mind,
wise in the face of future past/

maybe it is unlearning judgments & self hates
that weren't yours to make in the first place.
honoring the inherited & uninheriting/
laying to rest what has no place where you're destined.

seems everybody's saying love yourself/
nobody seems to be showing you how/

& either nobody can,
or everything already is/

gnosis/ no se/ yo se/

the heart knows what the mind reasons/
the soul needs what the heart feels/
& the heart needs the body that holds it
like it does the will of your spirit/

you need what you need
to see what you don't/

to know some things
you're better off without/

it takes what it takes
to be what you feel/

to shed the callous
& reveal the tender/

to call this being
your self/

a change of heart is allowed/

some suited walker waltzes down the avenue before they stop
& turn about face around midblock. how many steps it took for
what struck them to strike/ for them to remember what they forgot,
recalled, come to their senses or change their mind, who knows/

perhaps a misdirection,
sudden change of heart?

my best friend texts/ she's going through this break up/
years behind them both now this guy calls the relationship a waste
of time/ he wants something that isn't of her to give or for him
& she can't believe it's happening/ not because she didn't expect it,

but because there was a part of her that always saw it coming
& still let herself see it through just to know
what she already knew/

some ways down the block I stop. and I swear/
how people change when they don't get what they want/
how clear their face & naked the reveal/
ask myself what it takes/

how long do we know something
before we let ourselves believe it/
how far do we go knowing
the truth before we turn to face it?

no one has your eyes/

look back & you'll find

what you go through becomes
what you see through
& there isn't a thing you go through
that doesn't also go through you/

we're made from what we're made for/
as you are what is yours to face/

look around

no one has your eyes/
no one sees what you see
even if they see it too/

your body matters/ your height matters/
your size matters/ your depths matter/

the difference in your experience
& how you catch light matters.
your views matter. where you come from/
your texture/ the way you feel/ what you feel
how you feel it/ all matters/

because you are
what is yours to bear
& yours to bare/

look in/ see with eyes closed/ know yourself there

where you are is why you are here
where you are is why you are there

one soul two skins/

the gravity was already there between us/
all we had to do was look up/
the rest fell into place/

& what can I say?
saw something in you
that looked a lot like me

I can't explain how I know what it is but
sometimes I hear you speak & I swear
I know you from before/

we were once *us/*

can't say why we're here,
I just *know* this is why/

you leave me so full
I feel I am something of yours/
not lost or waiting to be found/
just here at the right place right time/

& it just might be kind/
to stay a while no?
learn what it is.
hear it out.

try to make sense
of one soul
in two skins?

drift/

earlier I pulled what was left
of your touch & offered it up

all along the hudson shore

you find all this stuff that has no place
where the river flows

plastics glass and clothes
once known to some body

such things lost in the current
scattered perhaps deliberately thrown

or such abandon a mere accident
swept up by some vicious change of wind

who knows however it happens
whatever it takes

to not want your memories
with someone anymore

whatever it takes
to take your skin off

by the time I write this
it hurts to write

my fingers throb
all too rough to make a fist

tough from the way
I couldn't keep us

sure as rain/

sure as rain some people usher in storms
and leave you in a fog. clouded
importantly so you can learn clarity/

to let pass what won't last and release
the want of trying to hold still the hurricanes/

sure as rain, some storms come as they came,
but ever after nothing is quite the same/

the way it takes a name to show you
what you're made of/ doesn't end
where it was written/

it takes what it takes/ hours & days/
trials & tribulations to unveil
how being is becoming is revealing/

all these faces & names, come and gone,
only to return and talk to me like they never left/

been here through all of it just to see
who they are/ what they've become/

what they've been through
that brought them back to me/

breathe deep/

to go where the breath turns to tempest
& the calm of your quiet turns to rage/

to see what happened
& hear it out/

to meet where the echoes stop
& light fails/

& see why/
and whisper there/

you deserve shelter from the storm
even if the storm is you/

you deserve shelter from the storm
even if the storm is you/

leaving has a scent that lingers/

you have this air about you/
I just want to breathe in/
feel you in my lungs for a second/

but the sun sets so fast when you want it to last/
ripens the sky violet to black when you wish
the feeling won't end & I see you eyeing that clearing/

the soft violence of a horizon
over river waves in the evening/
I don't know if I have that in me/

to hold you close by moving away/
give you something impossible to chase/
hope we don't end where it all seems to end/

what it takes to keep you without keeping you/
from what you're looking for/ who am I to hold you back/
just to find out little big city dreams like mine only fly on paper/

the way those little birds you draw when you don't know
how to draw birds always seem to know where they're going/
I know that light in your eyes/

what can I say when
I catch myself looking at you too long/
I'm high/ I think I'm falling/ I think I'm flying/

ask where to next?

oil on canvas of Icarus between worlds/

strange how a fine line makes such a world
of difference in the juxtaposition of things/

what could the ocean & sky/ day or night be
without the fragile horizon between them?

tell me there isn't a certain danger in being the grey
in a world so black & white, it's neither/

a certain cruelty in either or's & having to decide.
day or night/ dark or light/ this side that side/ *choose*

can't the horizon belong to both ends by belonging to neither?

see I've caught what becomes of clouds that don't make it
over the city across the river by twilight/

torn apart & left to the hungers of the night/
hanging somewhere in the middle of burning & fading/

like I am

torn/ between a deep need to disappear/
& craving to feel seen.

yielding/

perhaps the bravest thing you can do is stay
long enough to see the end you fear
may actually never come/

perhaps the most courageous thing you can do
is walk away before you become the very end
you promised you'd never become/

where you are is why you are there/

black bird flies into twilight
& I dream about where it's going/
where the other end of evening resides
that keeps everyday from the odds of never ending/

if ever I'd see that bird again/
would I know it as the one I saw/
tell it apart from the one mama shot as a girl/

upon the river, one's figure & form ripple in reflection/
I wander about the body/ wander about this skin/
about these hands and feet/ the tempests
at our fingertips/ every loop, radial, arch,
& whorl different/ all this world we are/

would I ever see it again
if I ever see it again/
if ever I were a bird
in another life/
would I know it/

know me as the one I was/
dreaming the same dreams/

if surrender was an element/

earlier I was thinking about something you said/
and how so much of what you've said has become what I say/
and I can't help but shut my eyes because I kind of hate it/

I open my eyes & watch the waves do what they do/
wonder, what are waves anyway. the sun breathing, a mirror?
the face of gravity/ the shape of wind/ an effect of butterfly wings/
a million eels whipping and lashing where the rivers meet the sea?

how water bends/ violet clouds into neon/ overcast skies into
mercury/ and transmutes sun into gold/ why it is so startling to
hear waves get louder but so peaceful to watch them rage/
what about it feels so good to jump with a big one or have it knock
you over/ let the salt have its way with you/ catch a current steal so
much from under your feet & heal/ why it seems to know exactly
what it's doing & where it's going/ I don't know.

I was thinking about the way water could be so many ways/
where there's water there's life, that saying/ the nature & texture
of something that can be anything but is what it is everywhere/
& anywhere/ liquid. solid. in between. cloud. breath.
all the colors under the sun. black in its absence.
clear as white light. all the things. all at once.
flirting/ kissing. not much different than us
when we were still one. so much
before we are right about who we are.

if surrender was an element it would be water/
& seeing yourself translated and welcoming the language
no matter how foreign the tongue/ seeing yourself change
with the life it gives/ slowly becoming the other
and letting it happen. maybe that's love.

which is totally something you would say.

all at once, it's already happened/

catch the moon bathe
in the failing light of day
as what's left of the flame
watches her until she's all ours/

to breathe & to think
our lungs throw caution to the wind
only to become the storms that bring
falls & springs, ruin & revelation/

that the sun you rise with every day
is the same sun every one every thing
every breath since the dawn
of the first day has also set with/

& not at all.

gone but never forgotten/

one man sits at the shore of a busy sidewalk
behind a cardboard sign. sunset gold pouring down
the avenue behind him. all he needs is three dollars
for a pizza & something to drink. the man says
he knows he's a worthless piece of shit
but all he needs is three dollars for a pizza
& something to drink.

three days ago, at her manhattan apartment,
an icon was announced dead. suicide by hanging.
can't say her name without people saying, *it's a damn shame.*
today, another suicide by hanging/ another damn shame.
soon, another big name/ another headline & more names/
some known, even more unknown by the year's end/
this & that about mental health trending/
more talk about what needs to be done/
be kind, seems to urge everyone/ *call your beloved/*
call the strong ones/ you never know, they say, over quotes
& RIP's under black & white imagery, retrospectives
& memories and public empathies all over the internet/
as the living name the way the departed lived their lives/
all they took for granted and left behind/ it would seem
the dead are most alive again before they're left to die/
gone but never forgotten/ in their return to the silence
where every living soul has something to say but them/

on the ride home, some kid tries for change/ a narrative in vain/
the sleepers sleep, the dazed and tired dream & drone on their
phones from whatever their days were, only so few looking up/
seems people are softer with those who are dying,
but we're all dying & life is hard/
a young woman cries across me/
who knows why/

the train goes on/

reading/

strangers on the train
who don't have eyes for anything but the page
of what book they're reading impress me/

they don't break for what stop it is/
whether who is to blame for the way we're stuck
between stops is in our car/

they don't check who texted them/
if the man's voice pleading for change matches his face/
if the girl who wears the floral docs *would wear the floral docs*/

or what I look like
reading them/

change/

man begs for change
but everyone
keeps giving him money/

saturn devouring its son/

you never know what someone is going through/
we hardly know who we are/
you never know underneath it all/
we're more afraid than we let ourselves be/

but who am I/ who am I/ who am I/
to judge a mask I wear myself?
you never know/ the faces/ people put on/ the walls
they put up/ just so they can take on what comes/

look around/ everybody's putting it on/
& nobody's looking.
nobody sees it but you/ the way
these faces we make, they do stay/

& the years do reveal us/
for all the faces we've made/
every wrinkle we've been/
we were born with/

as the future past eats our days/ Cronus devours
its children/ God eventually does the same/
& this life is merely the part that happens
when you're in between its teeth/

the whispered prayer a mere plea/ saying
whatever it takes to make it make sense/
to make it stop/ mouthful of tears/
trying not to scream/ swallow cry into quiet/

& call it triumph/
grace even, the chance
to see another day/
& do it all over again/

leap of faith/

one's mouth can be more sky than sky/
a tongue can carry more views than a horizon/

you can hear someone's wings/
the splendor in their unawareness/

hope they catch it/ the lightning noiseless
in the distance/ show them where to listen/

like a sparrow, they still have to learn
the way wings come together one feather at a time/
each feather, on their own/

one can see it all happen in the sky
of their mind but they won't know what it is/
until they leave the nest & risk their shape
to learn what the clouds already know/

the way up begins down here/
the way to heaven begins on earth/

the way grace takes falling first.

heaven forbid/

heaven forbid you end up in the middle of a sky
that ends exactly how you saw it coming/

the further I plummet/ into the depths of us/
chase the echo as far as our story can reach/
the more I find there's a certain cowardice
in flying away from rock bottom/

in bracing yourself for impact
like it'll make a difference or save you.

heaven forbid you didn't see this coming/

so you've never been there/
so it's different & it's taking everything/
to talk through how you want to stay
& run away at the same time/

so it hurts & it's dirty, this discomfort
& growing pain/ so it's not at all
what you've known or seen/

oh it's terrifying
& you're in the dark here/

so this is the work?
this is love?

yes. this is love.

& you'll never know it
only chasing beginnings.

mother of moments/

fall with what falls in you & you'll find the kid
who wonders where the sun sets never left.

in a blink I glimpse where I was first
before becoming this/ words still were what they meant/
or at least gave you very little reason to question them.

difference did not matter then, not nearly as much
as just speaking what you liked rather than caring
about whether or not you weren't liked.

sharing the same favorite color was enough to call a bond
chemistry & in spite of complexion, everyone was a friend
waiting to happen/ wasn't even a thought/ not a worry
in the world about what skin meant/ not a worry
in the world about what anything meant/ only curiosity.

perhaps nostalgia isn't a craving of our youth
because we were free then/ but rather a longing
for who we didn't have to be yet/

an age where being oneself wasn't just a game
of sacrificing change to buy your way out of sameness.

no I don't look back for nostalgia/

we're too damn young to be so nostalgic all the time/
like the kid in me seeks the sun, I seek this moment.

the source of it.

The Mother of Moments.
Father of Absence.

what made us so possible
that left us so impossible.

who told the authorities that came to shape our lives
you must be this tall to be men or this thin to be women/
this body type or body part to be either/
this way to be their way/
this faith to be their faith/
this tone texture shade
or color to be beautiful/
and who told them before them/
and them before them/
and them before them/
all the way to the beginning/
through breath before breath/
blood before blood
became bloodshed
& the blood of our bleeding/
before such matters mattered &
became the marrow in their bones,
and that marrow became us.

fall with what's fallen/
& maybe you'll find what came before is still there/
our ancestors, still children somewhere.

& maybe there is a chance for us still/ if we spiral
our minds sharp enough/ we'll come out the other side/
where there is still time to whisper with these son daughter
brother sister tongues/ tender kisses for fists
and feather their fingers/

show them where the sun sets is a soft place
& it is nothing to be afraid of.

I want to believe/

warm as summer/
you sing softer than whatever secrets
God sings to stars that raise the days
& lays heads to rest/

you breathe into me your heat
& do in my chest what the sun does to wax/
& just like that I am yours just the same/

& I can't say
if you're trying to get a rise out of me/
or leave me in the dark with all
tomorrow seems to promise/

all those sweet dreams you speak/

the rain keeps us honest/

but we only catch the sky is falling
when it lands. & when it does the city speaks.
you can hear it in the panic and feet/
the stories only so few ever tell/ everywhere
we'd rather be/ under such chaos & density/
for a moment no one is alone on these streets/
cars honk and howl and the pavement
has so much to say you almost
can't hear the clouds.

the sun underground & all the colors in between/

that's the thing about when it pours around these parts/
when you're down & out in heavy thought/
waiting for the light to change or any chance to cross/
the sun underground & all the colors in between rise
to catch your eyes in a puddle by the shore of a busy street/
a rainbow glistening in the grit & gasoline/

her eyes set on you/ lost horizon blues

I watch you day dream/
sights set and moving over the unknown
beauties of this foreign day/ & wonder

which unlived life will take you from me/

I look at you & ask myself why/
what do you want really?

are you here for me,
or are you here for me/

here for yourself/
because you want to be/

or because you think
you are necessary?

shame/
we don't get to see
how our lovers look at us
when we're not looking/

shame/
they'll never get to see it either
& we'll never know/

what they see/
or how our lovers look away/

only what they say/
only what they don't/

we're here & then we're gone/

don't be here if you're not
going to be here/

all of this could've been anything else/
anything could've been anything else/

could've been me/ could've been you/
could've been anyone/

but of all we are before we are gone/
we are here/ so be here/

or be gone/

nothing to see here/

how much must I take off/
how high must the sink be/
how far do I stick out my ass/
how much must I make up/
raise the stage/ raise the bar/
what do I need to say/

how loud/ do I speak/ quiet down/
to be seen & not be left on seen/
how much must I put on
to seem like me/
how naked must I get
before you see me/

be me/
how bare/
before there's nothing left
to see/

content content content/

all these impressions & no one's impressed/
all these faces & I don't know who anyone is/
all these likes & no one likes themselves/
all these followers & we're still lost/
got a sponsored wardrobe & nowhere to go/
all these clothes & we just get dressed for the internet/
fake off-guards to look authentic/

all these journeys & no one knows where they're going/
all this engagement & no one wants to engage/
all these stories/ all these stories to show everyone you're present
& you're not even present/ all this interaction & it's all an act/
all these comments & you only miss me
when the algorithm reminds you I exist/

all this art & no one gives a fuck who made it first/
all this consumption & no one cares whether or not they eat/
all these feeds & I still go to sleep hungry/
all these views & no one can see/
all this reach & we're still out of reach/
all this skin for all these hearts & you don't feel a thing/
all this to bring us closer & it's only getting in the way/
all these verifieds & what's real anymore but our inability to tell?

all this communication & miscommunication/
all this contact & we're still out of touch/
all these angles & no one has perspective/
all these accounts & no one's held accountable/
all these people & all we see is numbers/
all these numbers & they don't measure a thing/
all these numbers increasing, the joys of life decreasing/
& we're still numb to what matters/
all these insights & no one has insight/
all this influence & nothing changes/
all this content & no one is content.

all this content and no one is content.
all this content and no one is content.
all this content and no one is content.
all this content and no one is content.
all this content and no one is content.

all this content and no one is content.
all this content and no one is content.
all this content and no one is content.
all this content and no one is content.
all this content and no one is content.

all this content and no one is content.
all this content and no one is content.
all this content and no one is content.
all this content and no one is content.
all this content and no one is content.

all this content and no one is content.
all this content and no one is content.
all this content and no one is content.
all this content and no one is content.
all this content and no one is content.

all this content and no one is content.
all this content and no one is content.
all this content and no one is content.
all this content and no one is content.
all this content and no one is content.

all this content and no one is content.
all this content and no one is content.
all this content and no one is content.
all this content and no one is content.
all this content and no one is content.

are you content?

humble is a verb/

being authentic
is a lot like being humble/
the more you talk about it,
the less you are about it.

the art of being/ is being/

in a culture where all is curated/
to embrace yourself without performance/
as you are in public/ as you are alone/
is both an art & a statement.

who you are
is not about who is watching/
it's about being yourself/
regardless of who is looking/

you want so badly to be art/
but don't you see/
in all your unseen,
untrying & effortless being/

the art in the way you already are/

a devil knows better/ insist on the angel

this morning a devil took my face
& gave it to someone else/

the man who received this old face
had a feeling it did not belong to him/

in the dream I was both of them/

as the man & the one who knew/
we went out looking for me/

when we found a boy playing on a hill
very much in love with a young hunter/
I did not want to give him this face/
he was not yet either of us/
he still had a chance/

he was happy/

underneath/
I was too/

the boy flew after all/

as a kid I heard tales of a boy
who could've become his father & didn't/

& I'm still curious why we call the myth of Icarus
a tragedy of a boy who flew too close to the sun
& not the story of a boy who flew at all/

ether/

there's so much here
between us & between us

surrender to yield/

you will overcome your distances
when you get over the fear of being known/

you only ever reach the horizons
you learn to let go/

NIGHT IS INDIGO/

so you can feel it. what keeps you down during the day keeps you up at night & comes to light when the stillness unstills and the quiet unquiets. whatever rises when the sun nestles itself elsewhere knows exactly where to find my dark places/ however it crimsons the ether this particular tone of night and horizons the heavens does it to me where only so few ever see. crazy. the way moments are married before they ever meet & what comes together when you let it. the way things happen either way. all we'd been through to meet where we'd come to meet. I've tried my mind at colors I've never seen. to imagine all the colors in between. the way everything is what it is because of what is not, and I want to know what comes together to make colors dissolve when they are apart. I do forget what I was before delving into what we were. a past speaks and I listen until the black ceiling sparkles and touch is light in the dark. I reach into the noise and it gives me your name. miracle. the way you used to be up when I was. moving through songs before dawn, questioning everything too. I told you once I used to dream of a place time would stand still for us. so I could tell you everything between seconds & only we'd know it. no proof but the feeling that it happened. the moon had this way of giving us this. & I want to give you this song I'm listening to now, but I know sending songs is still talking. so I pull my skin instead. resist the confession. refrain from reaching through the glass to feel your name vibrate in my hands again. and between the fog ringing in my ears after loud music & birds warbling, I hear angels speak. they whisper cruelty is a wing with no feathers and catching all the falling things bound to crash. and grace is having to surrender to the idea of soft landings when you are everything but. and I know mercy means sleep is not defeat. but I know it's not insomnia when you must yield but want to be awake. & it's not that I don't want to sleep/ it's that I can't stand the thought of what I'd miss if I wasn't up for it/ what I wouldn't find if I wasn't losing my mind. but tonight, I'd give anything to fall asleep & not notice.

volumes & volumes of disquiet/

but the dark listens
where light thinks
it has things all figured out/

night knows what never sees the light of day/

all the moon's seen
and been through
& still it halos/

out on a limb/ from limb

from you
they take what they want
& leave only the parts
you can't make love to
without hurting.

fever/

& it's not what you took, but what you left of me/
the nights. the sleeps. the ease of both turned disease.
the thought. the feeling. the immeasurable quiet.
the way it longs for a voice. from inside out & begs for silence
beneath the chatter. it keeps me up. trying to remember.
the difference. between beginning & end. whisper & street siren.
between words said & words kept. what I remember & you.
keeps me going. further. deeper. like a ray of light cuts
through the edge of a door shut & needs the dark to see
the other side. like a question tries for an answer & a shadow
longs for the body. & a hand asleep knows where to find warmth
when your side of the bed becomes a resting place for spectres
colder than the moon. I dream of you. turning toward me.
reaching out. & I wake up sweating. alone in the light
of my own fire every time. it feels like mourning.
but I think it's only midnight.

triptych: a serenade of sorts/ an aubade of course/ & scheherazade

i. a serenade of sorts/

night is indigo so you can feel it
& I want to feel it with you/
every degree of your darkness
& each layer of your being
from blue to sunrise/

to know how deep your cuts go/
on the nights you can't sleep/
& talk about them & talk about our dreams/
& make music of the noise in your head/
& trace the flow & ebb of your moans and breath/

to be the soft light that breaks through your nightmares/
& the gold that helps you keep it all together/
to be there in the morning/ & be there
through the day/ to be there
through the evening/

and be there
& be there
& be there/

in every way/

ii. an aubade of course/

tonight is one of those nights/
where I want nothing more than
to be alone by your side/
listening to you breathe/

but too often lately I lie awake while you sleep
& I don't know why this feels like a portrait/
straight tumblr shit/

there are moments I think about kissing you up/
telling you what's on my mind/
take you where these nights have taken me/

but then I'd have to deal with you awake
hold your hand about why this time is different
for creatures like me/ & what this all means/
only to put you down all over again/

so I think about it/
& if I wasn't so embarrassed I'd be impressed
by how far and how long I can go not moving/
as I am by all the places I've gone and views I've seen/
while you toss, turn, twitch

and dream/

I can't remember the last time I got to know someone/
hours like these I miss it/ the late night texts/
autumn nights in all its confession/
blooming in the dark of someone new again/
but it's been so long I can't even
think of who I'd message/

so I think about it/

what life would be like if I were famous/
who would be in my bed if let myself be a shit/
how it would feel to have wings and soar/
what would come up if I turned my body inside out/
watch the tone of my thinking pour into reality/
who I'd be if I could be someone else/
what it would feel like to be inside someone else/
you as someone else/
someone else
inside you/

when you move/ my eyes fly shut
like morivivi, in case you notice
where I've gone/

& I could swear you do not sleep/
I could swear you're listening to me think/
I could swear you have been pretending too/
that you will turn and open your eyes
& say I heard that/

futures have flown through me & I'm still here/
between these sheets/ wondering if you ever mourn
what you might be missing/
this dark of me/ still so colorful
now more violet bruise than indigo blue
could be 4:00 or 5:00/

a small cold creeps through my body
voices rise and fade down the avenue/
the room fully blues and golds/
in a few hours you will say I look tired
& I will say I was out cold/

iii. scheherezade/

your lips taste like a name you don't speak/

tell me what you keep/
tucked away in that cold cheek/
what a stranger you are/
wherever sleep spirits us/
in my dreams you love me there/
but you don't love me in my dreams/

how the day breaks when
I kiss you & your skin tastes
like someone else/
what did you dream/
where did you go?

silence is many tongues before you hear it/

your skin is a lie/
I feel you here
but you are elsewhere/

I don't know what to believe/
your mouth says here to stay/

but your eyes don't
translate/

& I know a split tongue when I hear it,
body memory never forgets/

the way silence speaks
louder than words, body language
always folds where a voice breaks/

***secrets*/**

live under one's tongue long enough
& after a while, you get so good at being a secret
you learn to leave rooms like you were never in them/

one and done & never again/

now your voice lives in a drawer written pink on a paper note/
the date you wrote it to me a magenta fog/ literally,
it's blurred out/ the dried water spot on the page could be salt
or I don't know what, but I do recall the day/ you gave me your
favorite purple shirt/ was also the day you let me see you there.
lick your lips too nervous to kiss back/

promised nothing would change between us no matter
the changes/ what random little insiders riddle corner to corner
of the page/ I love yous scattered across the margins, water color
shore lines/ folds & creases on the sheet/ funny, we sat together
every day but all our notes ever say is *I miss you I miss you
I miss you*

naturally, I can't recall a sound we made/ your laugh
& the way you say your name of course matter more
than what I do because I can't remember the rest/
where the hell did the conversations evaporate to/
where did the date?

does anyone ever get back what they lost without finding they
never needed it/ without it becoming just another thing/ to long
for when it's late & wonder if it's too late/ to throw away on our
own terms & call it closure/ *is that closure?* to throw a past away
on our own terms and let it pass away/

call another broken promise another burned bridge/ another life
that did not serve us, another failed relationship/ do we ever find
what we're looking for without finding we're better with it than
without it/ better gone than taking up space for the rainy days
& lonely nights/ better, without our story becoming just another
one in the list of stories to burn & keep warm with/

the one & done and never again/

like the dark never happened/

you turn the light on
like the dark never happened between us/
come & gone as fast as you came/

leaves you uneasy how intently I wait/
to see where your eyes go
when your smile fades/

moon halo/

in the dead of night

the moon whispers to the nimbus a breath of light/
it says this dark place is nothing to get away from/

like a tempest passing through is already on its way
& trusts the trees can take the turbulence/

a past life is something to take on & hear out/
not curtail shush or shoo away/

what flowers if it isn't there for the rain/
who heals from the hurt if you aren't here for the pain/

how do you rise from damage if you don't with it
feel what rises before you lay it down to rest/

or catch what comes before you offer it over to the wind/
like the sky sees the moon's halo in spite all they've been/

let it go/ there isn't a thing you go through
that doesn't also go through you/

as the seasons do, what clouds
moves on & arises passes/

every breath is proof/

protect what I want from me/

when I survive my yawns till midnight they turn to poems/
another lung opens & a more honest angel takes the shift/
it says I am weak for what I want & just as guilty for it/
I mean truly, what do you feed the heart that wants it all?

I've got my hungers & I've got my ways of eating/
see these feral curiosities/ they do move me/
& this hungry heart has stopped for better or worse plenty,
but it does not quit/ the root & the belly. they growl differently,

see there are hours/ where salt and vinegar is the only tongue
that understands/ the only flavor beside tears & sweat that gets it/
and it's almost always after midnight, but always before
anything vanilla & best licked off the fingers/

and in these hours/ you don't want what's good for you/
you want what fucking tastes good,
even if you feel like shit the next day.

all shall be lost whether you have it or not,
an impulse howls, *so have while you can/*
all shall be lost/ but you've come too far to forget/

well to hell with it/ your ears the left side of your face,
congestion/ pain/ promise/ progress/ such spaces you've worked
so hard to orient/ your best foot forward, your best life/ your body
mass index/ your place here/ forget it/ you want to breathe ether/
you want to *become/ the space* you orient/ to be the heat
& the engine/ the coal & the furnace/ chimney & black smoke/
rain & cloud & thunder back down/ burn each story of this house
to the ground/ leave nothing to build from/ disappear
to a place you can hear the quiet machines breathing
& breathe with them/ beyond the heat/ where the clear hollow
of fire/ watches the world burn from within without/

& is this wrong/ is it so wrong I would go anywhere
to know/ do anything/ starve/ pale, shrink & shrivel up/
to reach the point before this fire started/ cancel
the hunger/ beat it to before it is born/ throw it up/
spit it out/ is it wrong I want to know where the hunger
comes from/ so I can never need again?
to never eat again/ to be clear of it/

see, when Prometheus stole the flame from God
He whispered it into our bodies/ into our hearts as penance/
but this ravenous animal can only feed on the thought of an old
lover's skin for so long/ before you start pulling off your own/
to feel the last time they touched you there & you felt it/

I'm sure we only get what we can handle
& I can't help but wonder what He's not giving me/
if what I'm missing would kill me right now or set us free/

if these honest angels only
protect what I want from me
by sending poems instead of your body/

all this want in the air/

& no angel is above blood/
no body is beyond hunger/

all this want in the air/
all this longing that can't be placed/

what are animals like us supposed to do
with all this desire. feed. sleep.

do it all over again?

needles & haystacks

you'll never find
your needle in the haystack
looking for it/

you must feel for it.

witching hour/

3AM only goes as far & deep
as you allow yourself to reach/

at 4AM I am afraid of only two things—

bumping into myself in the dark
& that the bleeding won't stop by dawn.

face it/

it should scare you
when you can longer
scare yourself/

you are everything
you are afraid of
all that terrifies you/

& the only one capable
of freeing you
from fear too/

& it should scare you
when you can no longer
scare yourself/

you only miss me when I'm cute/

you only want to talk when you want to talk
& you only miss me when I'm cute
you only want me when it's late
when the dark is getting over the day
always when I'm sure I've finally gotten over you

but it is too late to miss me
we're past the part where you ask what I'm up to
you want another chance like you didn't already
squander the one you had
& there is no chance left to give

so what would it matter now
that you see what we were
when you couldn't even see
what we had when it was happening
what does it matter now

it is too late to miss me

the sun in my eyes/

such little suns that rise over her smile
when she talks about the rain

the way she welcomes
what so many run away from

reminds me

I can't recall the last time it was day in me
& this reminds me the last time was also
the last sun that rose in my eyes

haven't seen it since

but looking at her speak such shine
I almost forget the dark times

downpour/

to hold onto this feeling
your hands over my wings
your arms around my waist

like clouds hold lightning
takes a storm to contain

a rain so heavy
I swear something in me
thunders when I must let you go

milky ways/

it is simply too easy/
to fall for the constellations on your skin/
to sink in the milky ways your eyes move,
take your hands & go over the moon.

muse/
don't you ever wonder how many lives
how many times we've done this
yes. everything about us is yes.

but I don't want to be the one
who loses the world chasing stars/
after all, they are dead
& you are beautiful.

I'd rather be here the whole night
learning how deep your name goes
than call looking through you seeing
& go the rest of our days wondering what you are.

eternity is a darling lie.
forever is boring.
infinity is for the lazy.
& one life is enough to love you.

hacking heaven/

weave past the ghosts, the miscellany of beasts
in the labyrinths of the magical & the not so much/
even if you don't believe in all the fantastical stuff,
you can't stay away/ neither can the theories & thoughts
of all as it is/ the witching hour makes poets & philosophers
of us all/ you know we owe our sentience to the stars/
I swear we wouldn't be here if our ancient ancestors
didn't lose a night of sleep to question what we are
& here we are/ still falling from trees/ spiraling down
from highs and rabbits holes we swore we never dreamed/
breaking night like heaven's ours for the hacking/

suddenly there are no secrets under our sun/
no mysterious phenomenon that isn't also obvious/
no luck only angels/ no past only memory/
no future only dreams/ no now only breathing/
& chances are we've always agreed/ chances are
miracles & to have met in this life is one of them/
I mean, of all the universes, us here/ what could be truer
than this which is so clear it eludes us/ so *there*
when no one is looking & still so real you could feel it/
what could prove gravity & disprove time
like the way we'd come together/
as if we were never apart/

& what is love if not the little things
that remind you to dream & leave you breathless/

what is love if not an endless conversation/
& a conversation should feel like breathing
never like holding your breath.

story untold of Icarus & Ariadne/

when you know you know/
& all I want to do is run away/

I can stay on this island forever with you
& that's exactly why I can't stay.

not the one/

come back
when your heart is broken/
I want to be the one
not the one who does it/

you are the one who chooses/

man looks in the mirror & sighs/
boy you've changed/

another midnight sun underground/
facing the train window/

& I don't know what it is
about being able to choose
what to look at/

the reflection or through it/

that feels like something
in it is there for us/

the need to know is a nightmare/

I can't help that I want to take a good thing & break it.
see what's really there. if there's room for me after all.
if what's there for me is for me, even when I'm not sorry.
it's just a feeling I can't shake. the need to know.

I destroyed us for a poem/
it wasn't very good, but neither were we/
wasn't my favorite either,
but then I knew.

what you were.

runner/

the day strips us of our wings/
denudes us of all we've done & become.
& it's too much/ having to let go of what I've picked up/
& pick up where I left off/ like what fell away
is still me. like I am what I was.

see, I've run away from myself enough times to know/
you always end up right where you started.
but you can pretend. suppress. every fatal curiosity/
redirect them. turn away from who you've been,

promise you've turned it all around/
swear you're different now/ do this enough
& the blur becomes clear. the world begins
to make perfect sense in our nausea.

but you can't run away from who you are/
you just learn to stand in solidarity
with what you've done & who you were
when you were the one who did.

you just learn how to be you
without having to be sorry.

again & again.

half-light prayer/

I call the angels
& they keep sending ghosts/
they say/ they don't know what to tell me/
until I learn to let go/

you can't keep nursing nostalgia
& wonder why it haunts you.

nothing is silent/

one is so many voices all at once,
some words just don't need words/
endless is the tongue before you speak/

lest you miss the hymn in your unawareness.
listen to what's calling from within/

you don't get to move with the muse
if you can't see the grace in her movement/
or hear the music in her thinking within yours/

can't you hear it/ the dark is for your eyes only/
don't you feel it/ how everything rhymes

& nothing is silent.

for all I've missed looking for it/

a quiet I can claim my own
a calm to call home
a place I can disappear

company in the safety of alone
the kind who just know
peace with what's there

this. here. a here so now
so real it's like I'm not even here

a silent wilderness only I can hear
a story only breath can tell

you. like I'm not even there
you. being so damn yourself

the quiet of your presence
the loudness of your absence

the nature of your being

I grow for you/ that's how deep/ that's how much

hands that undo the weight of your shoulders
how they melt the world away

a whisper that unravels the knots in your wings
a breath that leaves you breathless & breathing deeper
levitating in touch floating in kisses unbound & winded

let yourself dream in spite of
the nightmares you remember/

what you sleep on
wakes up in another

don't sleep on your magic
it just might dawn on somebody else

& you just might wake up
in someone else's dream

anxiety again/

a part of me dies when we are not talking/
I worry the last time we spoke
will be the last time we spoke.

service: searching...
message: seen

anxiety again

patience/ madness

nobody gives a damn
where you're going
until you get there/

but patience looks a lot like madness
to those who can't see what you feel
on the other end of your vision/

these sights you've set,
they may not see it yet/

the many suns we are before it sets
as we are moons & moons after/

how many days came and went
into every sleepless night or what it's all for/
the heights from here or the lows/

but they'll get it when you get there/
& this is what it looks like,
getting there/

you may already feel sure/
but you still have to get through
what you're going through
to learn what you already know/

night falls to remind us
we're bound to rise/

pride/

some people care so much about making it
on their own terms they don't make anything at all/

over thinking the damn thing
will kill you before the damn thing ever will/

more's been made with less heart/
think of what's in your hands/

let it go/

five minutes or five years/

hold dear what's yours to hold, dear/
feel what is yours to feel/

whether or not it matters
in five minutes or five years/
forget it/ forget hurt/

suffering is beside the point/
not suffering thoroughly is the tragedy/

feel what you feel/
have the heart to have your heart/
how it is as it is/

allow yourself to be
in what you're going through/

you live the truth you need
as you choose the light you die for/

until you don't need a metaphor
to feel alive anymore/

guilt is a sword with two hilts/

& there's probably
a reasonable explanation
for every dagger in our backs/

the thought of who I've hurt
pains me more than getting
hurt myself/ but I can't stop/

so if you ever find me
with a sword through my chest,
leave it there, I probably deserve it/

kills me more to take it out
than it does to let it rest/

beauty & the beast/

what I've seen & what I've done/
wouldn't put a damn thing
past anyone.

what I've seen & what I've done,
I don't need demons/
my humanity alone scares me.

my only hope:

that you don't love me less
the more you learn who I've been
without you/

the end again/

go ahead/
remind me of those long unforgettable moments we had,
those flickers we see in places we have & never been to.
let's pretend to reminisce, give nostalgia a kiss
so never again do we have to call each other up
when the sun falls and have to think about this.

not when we're standing naked waiting to get dressed,
or tracing every inch our lips have been
with our fingertips. so we never have to beg
for another minute of what we claim
we wouldn't be able to live with
if it were something we'd missed.

come now let's just get it over with.
come just the way you used to.
the way you always do. every time.
this will be the last just like the last
and the last before that.
let's end this like we mean it/

again. breathing in the smoke
and scent of something certain—
unquestionably questionable.

tempo/

yeah we fell together,
but at different speeds/

& really what does it matter in the end
if we don't meet the same end
at the same time?

sometimes where you fall isn't how you end up/
we get high but never to the same place/

you always get there first/
you always finish first/

CHRISTOPHER FERREIRAS

a poem is a promise no body can keep/

it's easy for a poet to muse
about the moon you deserve
when they're not
bound to give it to you.

the moon never answers either/

told the stars about you/
they didn't say a thing/
that was all I needed to hear/

I shouldn't be talking to stars no more/

ghosts never answer
when you got questions
only when they're cold/

let's be real/

the moon never answers
& that alone says something.

depth/

it's always nothing
when they don't want to talk about it/

but of course/

what you feel is never that deep
to those who rise from the way you drown/

day breaks us in/

what can you really tell me I haven't already told myself/
I've expected different & made peace with disappointment
so many times it never lets me down.
I've waged wars against myself & learned to shake hands
with what breaks me so no one can/ & mark my words,
I don't disappoint in my needless ways.
I want nothing from anyone, but patience.
and even then we're on a first name basis/
unexpectation, rejection, doubt, fear, failure,
anxiety & me. and none of them can tear me down
the way I've torn at my own name.

see, I know all this hope shit is half cruel.
the positive quotes don't work on me.
there is no mantra to change reality.
I've hoped nights into futures into endless nevers
only to watch things change whether I prayed them away or not.
I've hoped all the way from hell to high heaven
and stood over new day having sworn I'd never make it.
& there is no way you can hurt me I haven't hurt myself.
see, I keep my enemies close, not so I don't forget they're there,
but so they don't forget I am here. & they never fail
but neither do I. because I know what it is, I know who I am.

& you can't do a thing to me I haven't done to myself already.

I break my own heart a million times over
before anyone could ever get to it

& just like that/ no one can pick me up
the way I've learned to stand on my own two feet/

so if someone must break me,
I won't.

como/

tonight & tomorrow are only a dream apart
& here I am sundown to sunup

while you sleep/

how is it you're the one who did me wrong
& I'm the one left restless?

DAWN/
/dôn, dän/

salutations, old friend. I've lost track of how many lives I've watched you rise. the feathers I've shed and days I've fallen through just to find myself risen again like the warmth between blues. and in this lightness of midnight's pressure subsiding, the zero hour blur returns again to quell the chaos of questioning what is not for me to know right now. and it's a certain tranquility that comes with hearing out the noise. losing your mind a while. finding it was never lost. from up here, it's clearer than the cloudless sky/ if it wasn't for the sleep in between it'd all just be one long day. but then we'd never know that we don't have dreams. we are dreams. we have moments of lucidity. oh, what dawns when you let it & emerges into the cold light of day when you're listening/ how verily mourning comes when the night is done with you & morning always comes. you can hold on all night long/ wait up all you want before letting go of what never was/ the sun must rise/ and you just have to close your eyes & call it a day. like light is wherever you're looking, the here & now is whenever you are breathing. & no matter where you are you're always touching the sky/ you only need to open your hands & breathe. you don't need wings to reach the sun/ you only need to rise where it falls. receive it as it seeks your touch. it never forgets us, how far we've come, no matter how far it gets. never forget, in light of what you've seen & can't see anymore, you lose nothing to what's coming. welcome it. old friend, take from me what keeps me away. take it from me. what won't let me stay. let it be known. I did what was mine to do.

suspension/

night only knows what never sees the light of day
& I'm still trying to rise from how I fell for you/
the regret of how I never did/

what warmth courses through the blinds
tones the room that familiar shade of early & too late/
eyes wide open & I am still waiting to wake up from us/

awaiting to no avail/ grieving
the times my heart was a simple creature/

day breaks

& I never quite got over
being the unwanted one/

objects in mirror may be closer than they appear/

so where do we go from here now/
that turning back won't take us back
& taking back our damage won't change what happened?

history is real/ that's the shit you can't see while you're in it/
the past matters because it was once the present/ hard not to
resent this when you see, so clearly after the fact, how the words
you could've said seem to affect the matters that could've been
different/ the way *things* could've been different/

& on the long ride home, the ghosts seem to know exactly what
you meant to say/ but what the spectres don't tell you is that
memory is more poem than fact/ something you have to piece
together not something in tact & what you remember is most
pure when you can't/ & you can't/ recall what's past into present/
without dismembering the moments you do/

earth tones dull bleed and blend trees cars & towns alike
in the mirror/ the objects maybe closer than they appear/ or false/
like what looks real in retrograde is always false/ see there is no
ruin in the rear view/ that holds a greater truth than your
questions hold the destination/

it is not a map or a time machine you need/ but a feather
which draws the sky as spirals as it falls down towards the earth.
it goes in circles. sees all the sides before getting to the point.
& the fact is, every true feather lost to the earth
tells a story of a bird who found flight.

always picks up where you left off
from where you are now.

page not found/

I don't know if what we miss is really there/
or ours to catch/

I wanted you to be the one so badly
I couldn't see that you weren't/

an ember is proof of fire not failure/

perhaps/

that which lasts/
is always a shadow of how it started/

but that which did not make it
does not make it untrue/

& that which did not last
does not mean it was a lie/

that someone does not stay
does not mean they were not there/

no love is ever wasted
& no ember is a failed flame/

but a fire waiting
for the heat of another name.

perspective/

a love can outlast us
even if the relationship doesn't/

and there's nothing foolish about
wanting either end to yield eternity/

nothing foolish about wanting
love to last forever/

only foolish that we need it to
in order for the love to matter/

years are no more proof of time/
than a promise of security is proof of safety/

lasting does not validate time spent/
love is not your list of requirements/

not the boxes
or needs checked/

not your language, not your words
or your definitions for it/

but the feeling & the feeling
of those feelings/

the only measure/ how game
you are in the face of change/

the way you weather
the seasons together.

spent/

worse than a waste of time
is a lack of perspective
about where the time went
& what it all meant

the truth is always being told/

the body is always honest/

where you are being dishonest
with yourself is why
you feel so damn impossible/

but you can't hide from what you are/
you can't hide from what you feel/

honesty heals what hiding hurts/
& the hardest truths to tell
are the lies we tell ourselves/

like the tone of your actions
voice all you don't/

& the end tells all you did not
say in the beginning/

nothing is so quiet
you can't hear it/

the truth is always being told/
nothing is silent/

gold for a mirror/

when you meet this stranger/
tongue painted white & mouth full of words/
tales of wanderings long winded
& gone on for far too long/
promises of futures more promising
than histories known to you/

never trade your gold for the mirror/
the wealth of your being just to see it.

trust no shadow forecast
no banished sun
not even the eclipse foretold/

you need not another's hands
to see what to make with your own/
this is how they steal what is yours
only to sell it back to you/

make no sound of this treasure
& hear how they spend more time
showing you what they see rather
than showing you where to look/

do not despair
& do not rely on their eyes/

the God that knows your name
never hides behind men
who can't pronounce it/

sazon/

so many seasons, sembrando my roots to skull caps
just to hide the pajon/ cover up any trace
of where I come from/ a little rain did to my ends
what it does for Spring leaves & when you're new
to greña it's hard to see this as poetry/

there was a season
humidity was my enemy,
summer a sworn nemesis/
and then there was the season
I'd forget my umbrella just to feel
the clouds in my curls/

there were seasons I couldn't get
further away from Spanish
& the day I couldn't say cuando fue la ultima vez
yo me comi un sandwichito con huevo y queso frito/

the season I couldn't tell when was the last time
I had what I grew up eating & the season
I wanted nothing more than mangu
with cheese & salami/

there was a season anxiety swallowed my tongue
& the season I was brave enough to take it back/
a season Bachata made me quiet
and the season I began to sing along/

there was a season I didn't care
to declare myself Dominican,
y el sazon when I learned to dance
on my own terms.

you are not the trouble you think you are/

& it's all a softness to somebody/
these callouses, these crossroads in your hands/
could be the treasured by one who's been there/
known our kind of rough/

looks through the seeming tough
& sees diamonds soft to touch.

you are not the trouble you think you are/
you are a soft place to somebody/

I've never had to make my hands
softer for you to hold them/

like a feather never stops catching wind
even when it's lost to the wing/

you never stop being soft
no matter how hard you fall/

grace means nothing is ever lost
that can't again be found/

& softness is never lost/

you're a lighter place than you feel/
more tender than all this tension/

you wouldn't feel it if you were numb/

you wouldn't feel a thing
if you weren't softer than you feel/

the softest part of anyone/
is where they are most ashamed
& there is no shame in having shame/

so do not spare me your touch/
I will adore you there too/

no one is wrong for you/

you get a lot of people wrong
trying to make them the right ones/

you get yourself wrong too/

& that's the part
that's hard to recover from.

you're afraid of being seen/ I see you

when you want what you shouldn't have to ask for
& know it won't feel the same to have it after you do/

ask anyway & never forget/

it's not just anyone
who's going to look into your eyes
& see music/

not just anyone
who's going to look into your eyes
& feel your true colors/

maybe you can't make anyone understand
something they don't want to/
can't make anyone see
what they won't face either/

but you are enough/

some souls just haven't
been through enough to love you/

they won't know how to have you
& you shouldn't have to teach them/

it is surrender, love/ it means getting over oneself
to get closer/ opening up & letting in/

& you are not hard to love/
most people are just afraid/

of being seen through/
in their seeing too.

timing/

that one did not know how to receive your love
or what to make of the heart you gave
does not mean give up on love/

you have to know
you are wanted

despite whoever does not want you/
despite those who did not know how to have you/

that one did not know how to love you
does not make you impossible/

it only means you are more possible
than just any one can make sense of.

impressions/

& like that thing burning in heaven,
you are a light occurrence/

the grace of landing,
not the falling/

you do not have to be more
to leave an impression/

no need to force your being
into some way you are not feeling/

look/

even smoke casts a shadow/
even dust carries the sun/

I mean here we are,
something. somehow.

risen risen rising/

like dew from grit & gasoline/

risen risen rising/

against all that holds
us down/

right as rain/

the body has its own seasons & cycles/
through its own day and night.
phases to grieve & grow.
to rise and shine & hide.

there are gardens behind your face/
at times you open, at times you close/

it can winter so long one moment
& the next you're weeping
& you have no idea why
but it feels just right/

right as rain/

dust/

the body is never not letting go
of what is no longer you/

trust what falls away/
fell away because it had no place
where you are going/

believe what leaves releases you
& you'll never be left without/

how much is leaving you right now
& where aren't you yielding/

what return are you waiting for/

magic or something/

the right questions
can take you places
you've never been/

you say it's magic
where I take you/
the way I see it/

how your questions
answer mine/
you are something else/

you tell me who's the artist
when I behold in you
something only I can see/

I knew you'd do no harm to me/

weird thing, goodbyes/ I don't know what to say/
see you around, catch you later/ maybe never maybe some day/

dare I say I'm not sorry only grateful/ that bliss needs ignorance
& subtle is mercy that way/ what would ever happen otherwise/
if we knew wrong from right before going the distance/

dare I say it's okay to hear the gut & not listen to it/
what are years when the love is real/
or time when your hand's in mine/

naive as it may be to believe/ old souls stay young in love/
let my youth take the blame if this was a mistake
& we were wrong/ maybe we were fools/

on the same wave/ bound to part ways/
two shadows cast by the same flame/
one in breath/ slow dancing

in your room like our song would never end/
tripping into kisses/ begging forgiveness
better than begging the fates for another chance/

now here's the future taking us away/
the song still playing past our expiration date/
what can either of us say/

thank you for happening with me anyway?

stranded/

can't chase someone else's horizon
and wonder why you are lost
when you don't reach it/

pursue the dreams you have,
not what others dream for you/

love what is yours to love/
through your own heart/
never through the eyes of others/

you rise I rise/

not what lies in the distance
but the truth of going in the leaving
not the sun or the moon
but the harvest of feathers before flight
not your wings, but the way you wing it
not you reaching there
but you reaching at all

the radiance of burning for what you love

never the sky alone
but the solitude to find it on earth
never the heavens to steal its thunder
cast a shadow or seize its flame
but to help the sun spirit us
where we're destined

never the dream of flight
to leave this world behind
but to come back for it
& carry it with me

to remind you
every sun that's yours
to fall for is yours to rise from
& none can catch your sun

no one has what you see in the dark
no one can take what is yours to give

never the dream to give you the sky
but to see you give it to yourself

limitations/

not all freedoms you seek set you free/

some freedoms become the horizons that bind you
& only look like liberty until you see you never reach
what you need to keep moving in order to have/

and aren't you sick of it
drawing a horizon around you
& pretending you end there?

chasing worlds you once dreamed
to escape just to show yourself
you don't need what you wanted/

swear you only mean to make a difference,
playing the game just to change
every damn sameness from inside out/

they only serve to enslave you
further, some freedoms/
not liberate/

where true liberation never lies/

true freedom lies somewhere between letting go
& learning never to hold on/

untangling self worth from the horizon line,
the heights you reach & the lows if you don't/

where feeling is having & having is feeling/
& grasping is never keeping/

you are never too much light/
for the one who only has eyes for you

when a person whose gaze you cherish
sees what you've done/

glosses over your changes
& takes no pride in naming your triumph/

it is like a radiance is stolen from you
& an odd guilt to feel good/

a great rebellion of sorts
to take it back & keep it/

godforbid you love yourself without permission/

to know yourself
is to love yourself
to love yourself is to know
and not stop learning how

you've got to know who you are
in ways no one will ever tell you
you've got to know who you are
in ways others may never see

you've got to know who you are
so when they tell you
you'll know what they see is only that
never the whole of who you are

you've got to know there's a beauty in you
the world sees but nobody speaks
not because it's not there
but because nobody but you can

it is not enough to be so good
no one can say otherwise
you must be so good you don't need
one's attention to believe it

so good you don't need their eyes to see it too
so good it is enough that you believe
in the beauty you've beheld in yourself
& it won't matter who doesn't

you've got to know yourself
that you are worth knowing
in ways nobody else could ever know
in ways only you were born to see

dream/

if you were loved the way you love
would you feel at home
would you feel lost or found
would you feel free or bound?

if you were loved the way you love
would you love yourself?

& should this story come to an end/
would this love you found leave you
better after than before?

love should leave the heart better than it found us/

ever / after

you can be good at words/
and still not know what to say/

& isn't it always what goes unsaid
that comes to define what you mean?

the ends that tell all you did not say in the beginning/
how the end says what you meant & never justifies the means/

but you can be good at words/ and still
you need the quiet for a language to learn

nothing is silent
if you're listening/

everything's saying something/
what you don't have ears for/ what you don't say/

how we were good before each other
& we can be better after/

how what we had was a thing of beauty
& just because we found it together/

doesn't mean we are not beautiful anymore.

sleeper/ dreamer/ stranger/ friend/

we are all getting by in this life
so sure we know not knowing
anything at all/

please wake up,
bear in mind you are not the only one in this/
bare your soul you are not the only one in this/
& we give to each other by walking together/

the only damage in knowing the way
is that you have to go through it just to be sure/

the damage of knowing you are what you seek
is not knowing when it'll all make sense
& being yourself every step of the way anyway/

but even if we are alone in the dark,
we are never alone in the dark.

please be real/
there is no need to lie about where you are/
we are all looking for something/
finding our way/

no need to hide
where your feet are in life/
you are the other side
of what someone else is going through/

please remember/
no one has what you seek
because it is who you are,
not what you have.

self sabotage is not romantic/

the urge to get out of something
because you are afraid
you will ruin it if you stay/

is as much a fear of having
the thing work as it is a danger of losing
that which is worth having/

this urge will keep you on the move/
restless on even the best of days/
missing what's there looking for it/

& it keeps you going/ the wild stirring/
& you won't know when to stay until you stop
& let yourself have what you hold/

and feel it
through and through
and through and through/

this urge to get out of harm's way before it ever comes/
to leave the love before it ever sees the silk
in the dagger of your tongue/

will ruin you
before you ever get to break
what awaits if you stay/

this urge to get out of how far you've come/
only breeds escape & you'll never know
where the heart begins or ends running away/

walls or whatever/

you are deeper
than where one has chosen to stop looking/
further still than where they've turned away/

intricate & winding in ways
not just anyone can grasp/

like day is but a labyrinth
around the sun/

there is more
there is enough/

don't promise what you can't keep/

don't promise
you'll never hurt me/

you will fail.

promise
you'll let me hurt
in my own way/

that you'll be there as I do.

versus/

what eats away at you
is how you end up biting others/

who you are
depends on the hunger
you feed/

you are only at war
with what you don't surrender to/

armistice/

our greatest wars
are fought in silence/

hidden in plain sight
our greatest triumph

facing the day
after facing ourselves/

be there for your hurt/
your heart needs it/

sometimes
what burns has less to do with the fire
& more to do with how you treat the flame

the way you take the heat/

when a past life returns
let it find you *there/*

present. open, willing, patient,
to hear out the pangs

& feel out the fangs
of what is still torn/

be there for your heart/
where it hurts it heals/

& sometimes it hurts
sometimes you need it/

a good cry/

what you seek lies where you dare not look/

the beauty in sadness is
you don't see it until you let yourself

feel

how a feeling can eat you alive if you don't feel it
is how a numbness swallows you whole/

the unwanted feelings
will chase you until you face them

give the running a rest/ let them catch up/
take a breath & breathe with them.

so face them/

give them time & yourself space.
to catch up & make way/

for the unwanted feelings
will want you until you let them have you/

the unwanted feelings will want you/ until you
allow yourself to be in what you're going through/

& learn to want yourself with them too/

so face your fear/ learn its name/ love it out of you/

there is no pain you can't question out of hurting
& healing always burns before the fire becomes you.

blood/

you forget you are blood/
until you bleed/ until you see

what you are/
rivers & flows
all the same/

& there is no shame in bleeding/
no apology in blood/

ex nihilo, summer again/

the years do come & go/

the kids don't write their names on their notes/
but they know whose is whose
by way of which is not their own/

words are also a sort of skull & bone/
meaning, a marrow. the body of text,
a body spined not unlike our own/
every letter has already been written, dear/
undoubtedly like it has never been written before.

maybe it is true/ anything one could ever say
has already been said. what you want to do
has already been done, but never
by your hand & never again by you.

if it is your gift to give life to what you touch/
to turn a nothing into something
& contour blank canvas into body,
garden, ocean, landscape, or poem/

if you feel this gift
so deep in your bones
it hurts not to/

give & give
& do not hold back.

speak/

if you have not yet learned how to voice
what echoes in your throat/
& vibrates in your bones/

release your jaw & open your mouth/
unsilence the silence & let it breathe/
what you release releases you/

maybe no one will ever know
all that's had to die in you
so these words could live/

maybe no one will ever know you enough
to be right about who you are/

but you must let the virtue of any truth be
that speaking it does not kill you/

so speak your truth/
not to spare others your lies/

but to spare yourself
from having to live them.

stay radiant dear light/

every dark place is a chance
to learn a new flame/
to be your own warm place
before you are anybody else's/

take care of your fire
& sun your dark thoughts/
close your eyes & let the light in
shine out/

be warm to the coldest parts of you/
you're a warmer place than you feel/
warmer still than you remember/

don't let this cold world
suck the grace from your bones/
no matter who tries/

one's ignorance does not negate your radiance/
so never minimize or hide your brilliance for big eyes
attached to small minds. if one puts you through hell
imagine the violence they're living in with themselves.

stay radiant dear light/ no shadow
cast over you ever has to do with you
& that you attract the darkness you have a light for
doesn't mean they're yours to enlighten.
one might have the hands for the heat
but not everyone has what it takes to feed a flame.

stay radiant dear light/ regardless of what's fallen chasing you/
no sun is sorry for the way day breaks us in & turns to night/
no sun is sorry for a single soul that falls trying to reach it/

stay radiant dear light/
stay radiant dear light/

don't come any closer
if you're only going to be distant/

don't touch me if you aren't in it/
let me go if you aren't there.

I am a strange fire.
I only burn those who don't feel me.

dolor ajeno/

there should be a word for
a beauty that hurts.
for the beauty. & the hurt.

beauty like yours.
just might forget
it don't mean a thing.

beauty like yours.
just might forgive
it won't save us.

beauty like yours.
just might change me.

let go of what is not you/

less emphasis on self. more emphasis on being/
less mind on who you are. more heart where you are feeling/
less time remembering nevers & seeking escape/
more attention where you are breathing/

that you are not where you want to be
does not mean you are not where you need to be/
& that you are not who you want to be
does not mean you are not who you need to be/

you'll find what is yours to find
when you start believing you are worth it/
see, you wouldn't be where you are
if there wasn't something for you to see/

all is as it needs to be/

so don't change for a thing/
change as you are
not as others want you to/

let yourself
change as you will
not as others do/

not to better serve this world/
but because your spirit deserves it/
what only you can heal/

what you are no one can take from you/
as you are what is yours to reveal/

embrace this
& you will never stop
finding yourself/

no days off/

after all
what are we left with
but ourselves

you outlive all the things
you think you can't live without

you learn to outlast
all that does not last

how many times
you thought this was the end
and it wasn't

oh, the chances we take on anything
and everything but ourselves/

you forget what's in your heart
is also in your hands

& only you can do something about that/

you can have what you want
if you stop pretending
you don't know what that is/

you have it in you to live the life you want
& you have it in you, the life you want/

even the sun is in the dark,
that's why we see it/

& you wouldn't doubt yourself
if you didn't know you were good

you wouldn't doubt yourself
if you didn't know you were good/

there's a whole world in you/
get out there and find it.

keep me light, old friend/

let me lose what is not mine
so I do not have to believe I have it
so I do not need to nestle my peace
in something that is not there

ruin from my life what was not made for me
remove it from this moment
destroy my dreams of its future
take from me what is not mine

so I do not have to waste a single desire
or lose a single night remembering
what will not rise as I do

strip me of the feathers
that heavy my heart

keep me light

change as the day takes you/

it is a different sun that sets
from the one that rises

as you were from who you are
as you are from who you were

helios/

patience. Icarus
gathered fallen feathers from
dirt before he flew.

LET IT BE KNOWN
I HAVE MASTERED
NOTHING I HAVE
THE WORDS FOR

|| Christopher Hannimal

.